CASCADIA
GARDENING
SERIES

Growing Herbs

For the Maritime Northwest Gardener

Mary Preus

Sasquatch Books
Seattle

Envoi

In the name of the bee
And of the butterfly
And of the breeze
Amen.
— Emily Dickinson

Printed in the United States of America.

Series editor: Jan M. Silver
Manuscript editor: Suzanne Kotz
Cover design: Kris Morgan Design
Cover and interior photographs: Linda Younker,
    Bainbridge Island, Washington
Interior design: Lynne Faulk Design
Composition: Fay L. Bartels

Library of Congress Cataloging in Publication Data
Preus, Mary.
  Growing herbs : for the maritime northwest gardener / Mary Preus.
    p.   cm. — (Cascadia gardening series)
  Includes bibliographical references (p.   ) and index.
  ISBN 0-912365-98-6 : $9.95
    1. Herb gardening—Northwest Coast of North America. 2. Herbs—
Northwest Coast of North America.   I. Title.   II: Series.
SB351.H5P737 1994   93-42639
635'.7'09795—dc20   CIP

Sasquatch Books
1008 Western Avenue
Seattle, Washington 98104
(206) 467-4300

Other titles in the Cascadia Gardening Series:
Water-Wise Vegetables, by Steve Solomon
North Coast Roses, by Rhonda Massingham Hart
Winter Ornamentals, by Daniel J. Hinkley

Contents

Gardening in the Maritime Northwest

The maritime Northwest—lying west of the Cascade Range and running from British Columbia to northern California—is often called Cascadia. With its warm dry summers and cool rainy winters, this region offers particular challenges to gardeners. In addition to its temperate but often unpredictable weather, Cascadia is characterized by glacial soils, dramatic topography, and a growing population that is straining water supplies in urban areas. It is also a land blessed with both a full spectrum of native flora and ideal growing conditions for a vast array of non-native plants.

The Cascadia Gardening Series addresses the challenges and benefits of gardening in the maritime Northwest. Topics in the series cover both ornamental and food crops, and provide experienced as well as novice gardeners with up-to-date information and advice. The series authors rely on local knowledge, personal experience, and the counsel of regional gardening experts. Cultivation data is adapted to regional microclimates and soils, and recommendations for maintaining a healthy garden are tailored to specific conditions. Each book includes suggestions for drought- and pest-resistance varieties, landscaping, irrigation techniques, and plant selection.

The goal of the series is to help gardeners increase their knowledge, understanding, and enjoyment of gardening in the maritime Northwest. Please let us know what you think of this book, and what topics you would like to see explored in upcoming books in the Cascadia Gardening Series.

Cascadia Gardening Series
Sasquatch Books
1008 Western Avenue
Seattle, WA 98104

—*The Editors*

The World of Herbs

My adventures in the richly varied world of herbs began when I placed six stems of rosemary in a clay pot of sand with a plastic bag over the top. Each cutting survived, and so I started down an herb-strewn path. Twenty years later, those rosemary plants are still alive, and growing herbs has become a way of life.

For more than a decade, I have developed and managed Silver Bay Herb Farm, now a flourishing business in Silverdale, Washington. Although Silver Bay is commercial, its intimate scale gives me much in common with backyard gardeners. I regularly talk with customers and others who want to know how to grow and use herbs. If I am not in the shop, they find me in the gardens, leave messages on my answering machine, or stop me in the supermarket aisle for a few quick questions. Such encounters have convinced me of the need for a basic, inexpensive book about growing herbs in the maritime Northwest.

Most people first become interested in herbs for cooking. Perhaps a taste of fresh salsa flavored with cilantro, or herb-crusted salmon, or a salad of pungent herbs and greens inspires someone to try duplicating those great flavors at home. From the kitchen a path leads directly into the garden, where gourmets and gardeners begin growing their own herbs—first for the kitchen, later for ornamental landscaping or other purposes. For these reasons, I selected all plants in *Growing Herbs* primarily for their culinary use.

Succeeding with herbs that have both culinary and ornamental value starts with herb-growing basics—what plants need in the way of propagation and growing conditions. *Growing Herbs* will help expand your herbal repertoire as you learn to integrate cooking herbs into existing gardens and landscapes, or to design and maintain a practical, easy-care herb garden. You will find plans for specialty herb gardens, from baskets and containers to vegetable or ornamental plots, as well as tips on harvesting and preserving your herbs.

"Arugula to Thyme: 24 Herbs" (Chapter 5) details the specifics for raising individual herbs and integrating them into any garden design. You will learn when to set out your basil, what to do if your thyme blooms before you cut it, how to get rid of aphids on your rose geraniums without using poisons, which herbs to take in for the winter, and much more. An herb care guide (Chapter 6) summarizes month-by-month tasks in the garden throughout the four seasons.

Herbs have given me a livelihood, many friends, great and simple pleasures, hours of interesting study, and considerable food for thought. Like my children, they have become part of me, and I can hardly imagine life without them. My garden has been one of my greatest teachers, instilling patience and a sense of my place in the natural scheme of things.

As I walk alone through my gardens in the evening and note which herbs are ready to harvest, which need weeding or staking, and what the garden priorities for the coming week will be, my cares are forgotten. The soft greens and grays of the plants, their fragrances, and their subtle or bright blossoms against a background of water, mountains, and sky nourish my spirit. My hope is that you, too, will experience the sense of renewal, beauty, and joy that awaits in the world of herbs.

—Mary Preus

Herb-Growing Basics

Herbs are among the easiest and least demanding plants to grow. Gardeners are sometimes astonished by their success with these plants. "The mint just went wild," they tell me. "The cilantro keeps popping up everywhere, and there's a massive fennel plant in my backyard!" Many popular herbs such as chives, lovage, oregano, and sage are perennials that can be harvested for months or years with little more than an occasional glance their way. If you choose only a few of the easy-to-grow stalwarts and follow the growing tips in this book, you will have plenty of herbs for kitchen use, many of them rarely available in grocery stores. Most will reward minimal effort with an abundant harvest of beauty, fragrance, and flavor.

As you learn about the climate, soil, fertilizer, water, light, and pest-management needs of individual herbs, your success and pleasure in growing them will increase. The information in this chapter is general enough to apply to most herbs. Chapter 5 offers complete details for the planting and cultivation of two dozen specific herbs.

CONSIDERING CLIMATE

Herb gardeners soon become attuned to the special weather of the Pacific coast. The dry summers and rainy winters of the maritime Northwest recall the Mediterranean region, a source of many favorite herbs such as thyme, sage, and lavender.

During maritime Northwest winters, moisture-laden air moves in from the Pacific and meets the coastal ranges, producing a cloudy, rainy season that can extend from September through June. A winter might be so mild that calendula plants survive; another winter can begin with a snowstorm at Thanksgiving that kills off dozens of herbs and just gets worse.

A cold, wet spring can make it difficult to get any herbs planted,

1

but dry spells during the rainy season threaten the survival of vulnerable seedlings. In July and August, clear hot days are often coupled with cool nights, resulting in drought conditions and overall temperatures lower than in some places in Alaska.

Fortunately, the adaptability of herbs enables them to thrive in these varying weather conditions. Chives, fennel, lemon balm, lovage, mint, oregano, parsley, sage, winter savory, sweet cicely, and most thymes are completely winter hardy. Garlic, most lavender, and tarragon will survive our coldest weather if they have good drainage. Large, upright rosemary plants can be protected from low temperatures by covering them with fir boughs or blankets. Bay trees, scented geraniums, and small and trailing rosemary must be wintered indoors to ensure their survival. (See individual plant descriptions in Chapter 5 for more information.)

SOIL PREPARATION

Perfect soil—dark, crumbly, high in organic matter, well drained, and fertile—seldom occurs naturally in the maritime Northwest. Soils here are often shallow and rocky with hardpan underneath; even the best alluvial soils tend to be acidic and lack major nutrients. Luckily, herbs are among the most tolerant and forgiving of plants, and will grow well in a wide range of soil types and conditions.

It is often said that the aromatic or medicinal properties of herbs are strongest when they are grown in poor, dry soil. My experience has been that if you give your herbs fertile soil and a steady supply of water, they will produce lush growth with excellent fragrance and flavor. The cut-herb beds at my farm are intensively cultivated and harvested for at least six months of the year, and to maintain both quality and productivity, I constantly replenish and build the soil.

To give your herb garden the best start, ready your soil for cultivation with the fertilizer and soil mix formulas found in boxes throughout this chapter. Use the formulas as you would a recipe for a meal, measuring carefully at first, observing closely, making notes, and experimenting a bit as you gain experience.

Preparing Herb Beds

To prepare individual herb gardens, you can rototill to remove weeds and make a crumbly, even soil texture, and then line out herbs in rows separated by paths. Raised beds, however, are a more efficient use of garden space. Although they require greater initial effort, they produce high yields with low maintenance, improve drainage, and can be started earlier in the season.

Beds 4 feet wide by 6 feet long can be weeded and harvested easily from the sides and have room for a good supply of plants. Mark out beds with stakes and twine, shovel on soil from the path area around the bed (remember, a lowered path equals a raised bed), then heap on soil amendments (compost, manure, and fertilizer) as needed. Turn and mix the soil with a garden fork—not a pitchfork—rake the bed smooth, and you are ready to plant.

Neutralizing Acid Soil

To start, do a soil test to determine your soil's acidity (pH). Your county extension office can supply information about this (see "Sources," at the end of this book). The acid soils common to the maritime Northwest lock up existing and added nutrients, but the problem is easily corrected by adding ground limestone (lime), which is also a soil conditioner.

A pH of 7 is neutral; many herbs prefer a pH of 6.5 to 7.5. If your soil is more acidic, with a pH between 5.0 and 6.0, amend the soil with 5 pounds of agricultural lime per 100 square feet (10 pounds for clay soils). Use dolomitic limestone if your soil lacks manganese. You can apply lime at any time of year, but autumn is ideal because the lime washes in quickly once the rains begin.

Adding Compost

Compost, a key element of soil building, improves the structure and water-holding capacity of soil while it slowly releases nutrients and trace elements throughout the growing season. I have bins and heaps of compost in process year-round. The finished product is dark in color, smells sweet, and has an even, crumbly texture. With the current emphasis on recycling, the solid-waste disposal departments of many cities now provide information on composting, demonstration sites, and plans for compost and worm bins. Again, your county extension service can answer questions. Good-quality compost is increasingly available in garden stores.

At my farm, we work a 2-inch layer of compost into the beds as we prepare to plant annuals in spring—two 5-gallon buckets per square yard. We spread a like amount around perennials, scratching it in with a hand fork. For seedling and potting soils, we use the mix described in the boxes on pages 9 and 16. When a bed of salad greens or other short-lived annual is made ready for a second crop, we again sprinkle on a 2-inch layer of compost—and dig or till it in. When the compost supply runs out, we substitute organic fertilizers.

Using Green Manures

Nature's way of maintaining soil fertility is to produce grasses and other plants that return nutrients and organic materials to the earth as they decompose (the nitrogen cycle). Gardeners can use a similar method by sowing "green manure," cover crops that are turned under while tender. Green manures protect the soil structure from rain damage, prevent nutrient leaching, and help choke out weeds.

Crimson clover, hairy vetch, Austrian field peas, and small-seeded fava beans are all good choices for green manure. Winter rye, a very hardy annual, produces a tremendous root system and has the advantage of germinating in cool temperatures.

Sow these crops as the herb beds finish producing. The plants should be about 2 inches tall before cold weather arrives. Turn them under before they become tall and woody, and produce seeds. Wait at least three weeks before planting in the bed; decaying plants tie up nitrogen in the soil.

My successes with green manures have been mixed. Wild birds, especially crows, assume I am feeding them and gobble up the seeds or mow down tender growth. Hiding the seeds among basil and other annual herbs helps, and covering the seeds with old sheets or spun-bonded polyester row covers works, too. The cover allows light and moisture in, but keeps pests out. Crimson clover has beautiful blossoms; if it survives the winter, I let some of it bloom in spring, to the delight of garden visitors.

Working with Mulch

Mulch keeps weeds down, conserves water, and adds organic matter to the soil as it decays during the growing season. It also keeps soil temperatures cool and provides hiding places for slugs and snails, so wait until the weather is dry and warm, usually late June to early July, before you mulch. Grass clippings, hay, clean straw, shredded leaves, or newspaper all make good mulch. Black plastic (not really biodegradable) and black garden paper also can be used.

FERTILIZING

In addition to amending the soil, I fertilize my garden before sowing seeds and at various times as plants grow. A basic formula for all-purpose fertilizer can be varied according to ingredients at hand. I use a combination of fish meal or crab meal; bonemeal, greensand, and rock phosphate; and kelp meal (see the formula given in the box below). Besides the all-purpose fertilizer, I use two strengths of fish emulsion, one for new seedlings and one for maintaining maturing herbs.

My all-purpose organic fertilizer blend contains balanced amounts of nitrogen, phosphorous, and potassium (N-P-K), plus trace minerals.

Nitrogen is essential for all green, leafy growth, and is present in animal products such as fish, crab, and blood meal; animal manures; and oil seed meals, particularly cottonseed.

All-Purpose Fertilizer Mix

One batch of this mix weighs a little more than 5 pounds and is enough to fertilize 100 square feet, about the size of four 4-by-6-foot beds. If your soil is too acid and you have not amended it yet, add 1¼ pounds (1⅛ cups) of lime to the following recipe. The recommended materials are often sold by weight and vary considerably in density. For example, one cup of fish meal weighs about 6 ounces, while a cup of dolomite lime weighs 12 ounces. Weight also varies with moisture content and texture, so the amounts given are approximate. If you do not have a precise scale, use the cup measurements given in parentheses.

Ingredients

2 lb. (5 c.) fish meal or crab meal
½ lb. (¾ cup) greensand
½ lb. (1 c.) steamed bonemeal
1 lb. (1½ c.) rock phosphate
1 lb. (2¼ c.) kelp meal

Combine all the ingredients and mix.

Regular Solution Fish Fertilizer

Fertilize each 4-inch pot every two to three weeks with ¼ cup of this fertilizer, applied by watering can or turkey baster.

Ingredients

1 tbsp. (3 caps of a gallon-sized container)
  liquid fish fertilizer
1 gal. water

Shake fertilizer concentrate, dilute with water, and apply. One gallon will fertilize eighty 4-inch pots or six-packs.

Phosphorous, which is often lacking in maritime Northwest soils, promotes strong growth, healthy root systems, and earlier and better harvests. Phosphorous is available as ground or powdered rock phosphate, bonemeal, and, in smaller amounts, in fish and cottonseed meal.

Potassium helps plants form sturdy stems, resist disease, and overcome adverse weather and soil conditions. It also regulates the intake of nitrogen. Greensand and kelp meal are important sources of potassium, as is wood ash in lesser amounts.

Sprinkle the fertilizer over your soil and dig it in, or, to side dress rows, make a shallow furrow and apply 1 pound (1¼ cups) per 20 feet. For thickly sown beds of cilantro, for example, sprinkle the fertilizer evenly beside the furrow. Give individual plants such as mature basil about ⅛ cup per plant, then cover the fertilizer with soil. Water well. To give your herbs an extra boost, repeat this application midway through the plants' growing season.

I regularly use liquid fish fertilizer in my gardens to give plants a quick nitrogen boost. Every two or three weeks, use ¼ cup of regular solution fish fertilizer for each plant in containers or beds (see the fertilizer directions given in the box at the top of this page).

Many gardeners prefer to mix and apply a lighter solution of fish fertilizer every three to seven days, especially for seedlings. (For a recommended formula, see the light solution fish fertilizer recipe in the box on page 7.) Combine two tasks at once by mixing the solution in a watering

Light Solution Fish Fertilizer

Fertilize and water seedlings with this solution every three to seven days. Use approximately ¼ cup per pot.

Ingredients

1 tbsp. (3 caps of a gallon-sized container) fish fertilizer
2 gal. water

Shake fertilizer concentrate, dilute with water, and apply. One gallon will fertilize eighty 4-inch pots or six-packs.

can and fertilizing while you water. You can also irrigate tiny seedlings with a turkey baster. Fish solutions will keep for a while but smell bad; you may want to use any extra to fertilize elsewhere in your garden.

WATER

Although many herbs are extremely drought tolerant, most require a steady supply of water throughout the growing season to really thrive. Since nature does not always cooperate, some form of irrigation is necessary at times.

In the maritime Northwest, the rainy season usually extends through April, providing plenty of natural irrigation. In May and June, sprinkling seedbeds daily with a watering can or garden hose may be enough. From July through September, unless it rains, I usually rotate sprinklers to water the herb gardens as often as every three days. Do not wait until plants droop or turn yellow; water when the top 6 inches of soil have dried out. To save some watering labor in seedbeds, soak a burlap bag and place it over the bed until the seeds germinate.

Be sure to water the soil surrounding your plants to a depth of 8 to 12 inches. Water in the mornings (and evenings during hot weather) to minimize evaporation by the sun.

Within the past few years, drought conditions and water rationing have become everyday realities throughout the maritime Northwest, and many creative water-saving techniques have been devised, including water-holding polymers, soaker hoses made of recycled tires, drip-irrigation systems, and recyclable black paper mulches, to name a few.

LIGHT

Fortunate is the herb gardener who has a growing area in full sun. Most herbs do best with at least nine hours of direct sunlight; where it is too shady, they simply will not flourish. Don't despair, though, if your growing area gets only morning or afternoon sun, is shaded by conifers or other trees, or has dry soil. Just choose from the herbs for special conditions listed in the boxes in Chapter 2.

PROPAGATION

Herbs can be propagated by seeds, cuttings, or plant divisions. Starter plants are available at many herb farms and garden centers, usually in small pots and tray packs. This is often the best approach for herbs that are hard to start or find.

Starting Seeds

Especially for easily transplanted annuals, starting your own plants from seed is gratifying and inexpensive. All herb seed can be sown directly in the garden, but to get an earlier start and have greater control over watering and spacing, sow seeds indoors. With a sunny window or indoor lights, you can significantly extend the season of productivity. A small greenhouse or cold frame also opens up new possibilities. For example, by sowing basil indoors at three-week intervals beginning in mid-March, you can be harvesting in June.

To get started, assemble clay, plastic, or fiber pots and trays. Use a separate container for each kind of seed, since seeds germinate and grow at different rates. Six-packs are a practical size to work with; I also like using recycled tofu trays with drainage holes punched in the bottom. If you reuse plastic pots or flats, wash and soak them in a solution of 1 teaspoon of bleach per gallon of water.

A good soil mix for starting seeds consists of equal parts sphagnum peat moss and perlite, with a little lime added to counteract the acidity of the peat (see the box on page 9 for mixing instructions).

Fill your trays almost to the top with the mix. Don't skimp on the corners, since the soil level will drop gradually as the plants are watered. Sow the seeds evenly in rows marked out with your finger or

Seed Starting Mix

Derived from the Cornell "Peat Lite" formulas, this mix is good for seed germination and container growing of spring-bedding plants. Its components are lightweight and readily available, and require no sterilization. One batch of this mix fills about 20 six-packs (5½ inches long by 3¼ inches wide by 2½ inches tall).

Ingredients

4 qt. sphagnum peat moss
4 qt. fine-grade perlite (puffed pumice)
1 tbsp. ground dolomitic limestone

Mix the ingredients in a 5-gallon plastic utility bucket and add enough water to make the soil workable. Make sure the peat moss is well dampened during mixing.

a trowel tip, or just scatter them across the soil surface. If you wish to transplant directly from the tray to the garden, leave plenty of growing space between the seeds—otherwise, you will need to move the seedlings into larger pots as they grow. Carefully cover the seeds with soil to a depth 2½ times the length of the seed. Firm the soil lightly, and sprinkle the tray gently. Cover the tray with plastic wrap to hold in moisture until the seeds germinate. After germination, a pair of "seedling leaves" (cotyledons) appears, followed by sets of "true leaves" that more closely resemble the mature plant.

Check your baby plants daily to be sure that they do not dry out at the seedling stage. Give them good air circulation to prevent fungus diseases, plenty of light so the stems become stocky, and water them with light solution fish fertilizer every three to seven days. Within a few weeks you will have nice, healthy seedlings with two or three sets of leaves, ready for transplanting.

When the weather warms, usually in mid-April, get your herbs used to outdoor conditions by hardening them off gradually. Put them outside in direct light for 2 hours the first day, then bring them in.

Repeat this "out and in" routine for about five days, exposing them to natural conditions for a little longer each day, and finally leave them out overnight before transplanting to the garden. Otherwise the temperature change can stress the plants or the tender leaves can become sunburned, especially basil seedlings. For transplanting, wait for cloudy weather. Transpiration (plant breathing) is faster on breezy, sunny days, causing plants to give off water faster than their roots absorb it. This can shock and weaken vulnerable seedlings considerably.

Propagation from Cuttings

Vegetative propagation by cuttings is the method most used by commercial growers to reproduce perennial herbs. Some, such as oregano and thyme, do not "come true" to the parent plant from seed and therefore must be reproduced vegetatively; others, such as French tarragon, do not produce seeds at all.

I recommend the very simple method I used to make the rosemary cuttings that originally started me in herb growing. Test the "ripeness" of the stems you wish to propagate by bending them between your thumb and forefinger. Use them if they snap cleanly and do not wobble or resist too much. With a sharp, clean knife or clipper, cut 4- to 6-inch-long pieces of stem from the parent plants. Hold the collected cuttings in a plastic bag with a dampened paper towel inside until you are ready to plant.

Before planting, some growers dip the tips of cuttings in rooting hormone powder; it can be beneficial but is not crucial. Stick each cutting into a clean 6-inch clay pot filled with a rooting medium of half sand and half perlite. Tamp down the rooting mixture firmly around each cutting. To make a mini-greenhouse, bend lengths of wire coat hangers into arches over the pot; cover it with a widemouthed jar or plastic bag closed with a rubber band. If you can provide the cuttings with bottom heat from a heating cable or mat, so much the better.

In three weeks to a month, test to see if the cuttings are ready. Tug at one plant gently to see if roots are forming; if there is definite resistance, loosen the plant from the medium. A well-formed root system indicates that the plant is ready to be potted up or moved outside.

Root Divisions

To produce large plants quickly, make root divisions in the spring or fall. Slice apart the matted roots of creeping thyme and mint with a sharp knife or spade. Cut or tear apart root clumps of oregano, tarragon, and others. Fleshy-rooted herbs such as lovage form offsets, which you can cut off and replant. Make sure there are enough roots on each division, and water the plants adequately until they become established.

ORGANIC PEST AND DISEASE MANAGEMENT

One of the benefits of growing herbs is that most are resistant to insect pests and diseases. Exceptions exist, however, and they include some garden favorites. Over the years I have experimented with various organic methods to keep destructive insects away from prized plants. Organic gardening requires building healthy soil that grows strong plants and using nontoxic methods for prevention and control, beginning with cultural practices and resorting to strong commercial products only when all else fails.

Following is a brief rundown of the most common pests in the maritime Northwest and methods for controlling them. A word about diseases comes after this section. Look for more information on pests and diseases under individual herb descriptions in Chapter 5.

Herb Pests

APHIDS: Both green and black aphids are fond of dill, fennel, scented geraniums, nasturtiums, and other herbs. They can be a serious problem in the greenhouse and quite an annoyance outdoors.

Garlic repels aphids if planted among your herbs and edible flowers. Some gardeners report success with a spray made from garlic and hot pepper whirled with water in the blender. For severe infestations I use insecticidal soap, according to package directions, in both my greenhouse and garden. This contact insecticide, based on naturally occurring fatty acids, quickly breaks down and leaves no residue.

FLEA BEETLES: These tiny, black, hard-bodied insects hop from place to place, leaving small shotlike holes in the leaves of herbs, such as basil and arugula, and many vegetables. They live on weeds in and around the garden, so clean cultivation is one of the best ways to keep them in check.

Try covering susceptible herbs with floating row covers immediately after seeding or transplanting. These "miracle blankets" made of spun-bonded polyester let in light and trap heat and moisture while keeping out insects. As a last resort for really troublesome infestations, rotenone dust, made of ground plant roots, is the best organic control measure I have found. But use it with care; this broad-spectrum insecticide is harmful to beneficial insects, too. For best results, apply rotenone when the air is still, according to package directions. Rotenone biodegrades within 5 to 10 days.

SLUGS AND SNAILS: The bane of maritime Northwest gardeners, these pests adore basil, tender tarragon shoots, and various salad greens. I have even seen them attacking thyme plants. My neighbor complains that if you kill one slug, six more come to its funeral.

Again and again, people have asked me how to deal with these many-toothed monsters. There *are* ways to diminish the problem. Slugs and snails lurk in shade, so it is imperative to remove their hiding places. Clear away boards, boxes, piles of weed stalks, and other debris around your garden. Keep weeds down, particularly around the bases of perennials or shrubs. Keep your compost heap contained if possible. Mow the grass around the edge of your garden. These measures really help to reduce the number of slugs and snails.

Beyond the above cultural suggestions, I use several other tactics. Learn to recognize slug eggs, which look like small translucent beads, and squash them on sight. Go on search-and-destroy missions on cool damp mornings and rainy days. Outline your herb beds with wood ashes or diatomaceous earth (sharp, dustlike skeletons of prehistoric algae). In the evening, have beer parties for your slugs. Use nasty poisons if you must. Try anything, and good luck.

GARDEN WEBWORMS AND TOMATO FRUITWORMS: Both these pests are recent arrivals in my garden. Webworms twist the leaves of lemon balm, mint, and other herbs around themselves to make hideouts while they devour plants; fruitworms eat basil as fast as it can grow. The bacterium *Bacillus thuringiensis* (Bt) provides specific control for caterpillars when sprayed on plants in the evening according to package directions. It kills caterpillars when they ingest it, but leaves no toxic residue and is harmless to earthworms and other beneficial organisms.

About Diseases

Herbs generally are disease resistant, but specific herbs have occasional problems. Some mints are susceptible to rust infection; garlic might suffer from mold and rot. Check descriptions of individual herbs in Chapter 5 for descriptions of diseases.

CHAPTER 2

Planning Your Herb Garden

From ground-hugging thymes to 25-foot bay trees, herbs encompass "any plants useful for flavor, fragrance, or physic," according to the Herb Society of America. Countless herbs are used differently around the world. But in my experience, about two dozen herbs—the ones described in Chapter 5—are the consistent favorites of cooks and gardeners who save money and improve quality by growing their own.

CHOOSING YOUR HERBS

Before you ever buy a packet of seeds or lift a spade, consider whether you want to grow herbs for seasonings, fragrance, beauty in the garden, medicine, or a combination of uses. Begin to familiarize yourself with the appearance, growth habits, and ideal growing conditions of the plants you are considering. Visit gardens where you can see them firsthand (see Regional Destinations, page 80). Decide if you need annuals, which complete their life cycle in a single season; biennials, which will live two years; or perennials, which could remain in the same spot for several years, growing gradually larger.

The character of an herb garden is partly determined by the size, aspect, and soil of the site. A sunny area with moderately fertile, well-drained soil is ideal for growing the greatest variety of herbs, but you can work with a dry hillside, a parking strip, a shady backyard, a damp area, or gravelly spots. At least some herbs will grow in almost any garden conditions. If you have room only for planters, you can still succeed, as you will learn in Chapter 3. See the boxes on pages 14 and 15 for herbs that thrive in special growing conditions.

Incorporate water-wise herbs such as lavender, rose geraniums, flavorful oregano, sage, or common thyme to compensate for the periodic stresses of drought, seasonally low rainfall, and water restrictions experienced from northern California to Vancouver, British Columbia.

Herbs for Hot and Dry Areas

Herbs native to hot, sunny Mediterranean climates are well adapted to "hot spots" next to house walls, dry hillsides, and similar situations where other plants cannot survive. These choices for extremely sunny, dry areas also bring beauty and stability to the landscape with minimal irrigation.

Fennel	Rosemary
Lavender	Sage
Oregano	Savory
Rose Geranium	Thyme

If limited space is a problem, perhaps in a city garden, choose from herbs with compact habits such as deep green parsley or winter savory, graceful rosemary, or attractive lavenders and scented geraniums.

In some garden areas you may depend on evergreen herbs such as rosemary, sage, thyme, and winter savory as constants in your landscape design as well as in your cooking repertoire. Or perhaps you are looking for a ground cover to enhance ornamentals or complete a planting. Consider herbs that spread madly, such as brilliant nasturtiums or pretty creeping thymes—golden thyme, with its chartreuse leaves and mounded form, or woolly thyme, a handsome gray. Also, many annual herbs can fill your garden with short-term color while perennials become established. You can find the right herbs for almost any situation.

PLACING YOUR HERBS

Once you have selected your herbs and learned about the conditions they prefer, decide whether you will grow them in containers, your yard or vegetable patch, or in a separate herb garden.

Container Gardens

Many herbs are excellent choices for container gardening, especially when space is limited. This rewarding method of growing herbs also

Herbs for Shady and Wet Areas

Herbs of many colors, textures, and heights are ideal for those areas that are shady most or part of the day, and many shade-loving herbs can take fairly moist soil. In addition to the herbs listed below, numerous varieties of **mint** also like shade and thrive in wet areas such as stream banks.

Full Shade	Partial Shade	Moist Soil
Lemon Balm	Bay Leaf	Lemon Balm
Lovage	Chives	Nasturtium
Nasturtium	Cilantro	Sweet Cicely
Sweet Cicely	Fennel	
	Oregano	
	Parsley	

saves you the effort of maintaining a large garden. You can place your containers within easy reach of the kitchen and even make them portable. You also can control the soil mixture, watering, and fertilizing of individual herbs or of groupings with similar cultural requirements.

Any of the attractive containers available in garden stores and nurseries are suitable for growing herbs. I have had great success with herb gardens planted in old wheelbarrows and tires, too.

For organic growing, choose a quality commercial blend of organic materials and nutrients, or mix your own potting soil. Soilless mixtures have the proper texture for growth, but you must provide essential nutrients by fertilizing regularly.

To ensure good drainage, line the bottom of the container with clay pot shards or gravel. I also have used plastic packaging pellets in the bottom of deep containers, covering them with a plastic sheet punched with drainage holes.

Nearly all the herbs in this book are suitable for growing in containers, with a few caveats. Oregano and lemon balm tend to take over if combined with other herbs. Mints should be planted separately and the roots trimmed back often. Lovage and especially fennel grow tall

Basic Potting Soil

Potting mixes containing soil or compost hold their texture and fertility longer than soilless mixes, but do produce some weeds unless sterilized. Avoid using garden soil alone, as it tends to be heavy and poorly aerated, and hardens after watering.

In this formula, the compost or earthworm castings contribute good soil structure and nutrients, peat moss holds water and nutrients, perlite (puffed pumice) lightens the mix and provides aeration, and sand improves drainage.

Ingredients

8 qt. compost, earthworm castings, composted chicken or
    steer manure
4 qt. sphagnum peat moss
4 qt. coarse perlite
4 qt. builders sand
1 c. all-purpose fertilizer mix
3 tbsp. ground dolomitic limestone

Mix all ingredients thoroughly in a 5-gallon plastic bucket with enough water to moisten well. Peat moss absorbs water slowly; if possible, allow the potting mix to stand overnight so moisture is evenly distributed.

but can be appropriate for large-scale container gardens. Plant lists and directions for five specialty herb containers are given in Chapter 3.

Existing Gardens

The easiest way to begin growing herbs is to tuck them into open spots in the yard. As long as their requirements for sun, soil, and moisture are met, they will usually thrive.

You could plant mint beside a water faucet; sweet woodruff under rhododendrons; sweet basil and marjoram in tubs on the deck where they will get lots of sun; sweet cicely in the shade of an old apple tree;

lavender beside your gate; and creeping thyme along your path. What, no path, no gate? No matter. Plant your lovage at the back of your flower bed, the garlic around the roses, your tarragon next to the salvias, and edge the whole thing with 'Spicy Globe' basil for a gorgeous effect. There are endless possibilities for these adaptable plants.

Vegetable Gardens

Herbs can be incorporated into a section of your vegetable garden. For most home gardeners, one bed of 4 feet wide by 6 feet long provides ample space for annual herbs and allows for convenient harvesting. You might plant one-quarter of the bed with herbs such as arugula, cilantro, and baby dill, which can be sown in succession any time from mid-March through mid-September, perhaps in combination with salad greens. Group slower-growing nasturtiums, savory, and sweet marjoram, sown or set out in May and harvested until frost, in another quarter of the bed. Sweet basil—an herb to grow and use in quantity—might fill the remaining half.

Try grouping perennial herbs together within your vegetable garden. They will outlive your vegetables, and without some forethought you could end up with a sage plant here, a rampant mint there, and other herbs to work around in future seasons. Place all your perennials in one bed, or around the edge of the garden in a decorative fashion—voila! You have an herb garden!

Separate Herb Gardens

Separate herb gardens lend themselves to countless themes and variations. They can be almost any shape, whether rigidly geometric or softly contoured. Consult books on garden design for planting schemes (see Sources, page 87), but keep in mind that decisions you make now can always be changed. Half the fun of gardening is rearranging plants according to fresh inspiration.

Aesthetically, your garden will be most successful if you visualize how the mature plants will look throughout the seasons. As your experience grows, you will see that certain garden arrangements are more convenient for harvesting and maintenance, that some plants do best in a specific part of the garden, and that great beauty comes from particular combinations and juxtapositions of plants.

With their fresh scents and varied foliage, herbs can lend a delightful ambience to an area used for outdoor meals or conversation.

Herbs by Color

A spot of color—from a flower or a leaf—can add a wonderful accent to the greens and grays of an herb garden.

Herb	Foliage	Flower
Arugula	Deep green	Creamy white, light veining
Basil	Purple, burgundy	White to pinkish
Calendula	Light green	Vibrant yellow, orange; some have dark centers
Chives	Deep green	Mauve; white in garlic chives
Fennel	Copper-bronze, shiny	Pale yellow
Lavender	Grayish green	Lavender to purple; also pink, white
Lemon Balm	Yellow to green, or variegated	Tiny white; inconspicuous
Mint	Bright green to gray or variegated	Pink, purple, or white
Nasturtium	Medium green, variegated with cream in Alaska varieties	Wide color range: strong orange, yellow, red, cherry; softer cream, mahogany
Oregano	Medium green, variegated	White or pink
Rose Geranium	Medium green	Light pink
Rosemary	Deep green	Light blue, rarely pink or white
Sweet Cicely	Light green, mottled with white	White, conspicuous
Thyme	Deep or gray-green, golden, cream, or silver variegation	Light pink, less commonly red, white

Their subtle and restful colors are perfect for small havens that refresh and calm the senses. Place an ornamental herb garden where it can be viewed from the living room; position a kitchen garden close to the back door. If the garden will do double duty as a play area, sturdy herbs such as fennel, mint, nasturtium, rosemary, sage, and thyme can stand up to occasional abuse from children and pets.

By concentrating herbs in one area, you will be more likely to use and care for them. When you go out to pick a sprig of rosemary for your chicken, you might harvest a few nasturtium blossoms to brighten up your salad. Perhaps you will notice that the sage is beginning to bloom, that a slug is attacking your basil, or that a bit of quack grass is creeping into the chives. Fifteen minutes later, the situation is all squared away—for now, at least.

Herbs by Fragrance

Most of the following herbs release their scent when crushed. Those with an asterisk (*) are especially fragrant and give off scent more readily.

Basil: spicy, warm, and delicious; clove scent
Bay: lightly resinous
Chives: mild onion scent
Fennel: like licorice, especially the crushed seeds
Garlic: pungent and strong
*Lavender: fresh, clean, sweet
*Marjoram: perfumed, exquisite, floral
*Mint: refreshing, cool; fruity or citrusy in some kinds
Nasturtium: peppery
Oregano: warm, strong
Parsley: fresh, herbal, green
*Rose Geranium: remarkably like roses, heavily perfumed
*Rosemary: piney, strong
Sage: herbal, slightly musky
Savory: herbal, pungent
Sweet Cicely: sweet, licorice aroma in all parts
*Thyme: strong, medicinal, like Greek hillsides

CHAPTER 3

Seven Herb Gardens

CREATIVE THEME PLANTINGS

Herbs bring romance to a garden as few other plants do. Even ordinary herbs such as parsley possess special dimensions of history, lore, and symbolism. Grown as long ago as Biblical days, herbs are links to faraway people, places, and times. Grouping them together according to theme offers creative opportunities that engage the mind as well as the senses.

KITCHEN HERB GARDENS

Beautiful as well as useful, kitchen herb gardens are uniquely satisfying. When you grow and harvest your own food, you are directly in touch with the earth and the seasons in a way that has become increasingly rare. You take part in the natural cycle of growth, decay, and regeneration.

With fresh herbs just minutes from your kitchen, you will soon become familiar with their unsurpassed flavors. Like chefs at gourmet restaurants, you will no longer be satisfied with dried herbs that have lost their flavors. As your repertoire of recipes and combinations expands, using fresh herbs to make your cooking more interesting and healthful will become second nature.

Following are seven kitchen gardens, starting with a simple one in a basket, proceeding to four in planters, and concluding with two herb patches. From each you will reap a harvest of herbal pleasures.

Preparing Herb Baskets

To make a live herb basket, choose a sturdy basket and line it with a double layer of thick plastic, allowing an inch or two extra to extend above the top. Some baskets can be purchased with plastic liners.

Punch holes through the plastic for drainage, then cover the bottom with a 1- to 2-inch layer of clay pot shards or coarse gravel. Next, put in a 3-inch layer of good potting soil (see basic potting soil recipe in the box on page 16). Set plants in, bring the soil level to the top of the basket, and firm in plants well. Trim the plastic to the basket top. Water the newly planted herbs with regular solution fish fertilizer; water when the soil looks dry (outdoors or over a plastic sheet); continue to fertilize every week or two to produce herbs throughout the summer.

Herb Garden in a Basket

Plant List
2 basil
1 chive
1 sweet marjoram
2 trailing nasturtium
1 parsley
1 thyme
1 basket (12 inches by 12 inches by 6 inches deep)

This live herb garden makes a lovely gift for Easter, Mother's Day, or any special occasion. Choose common herbs from the list, or jazz it up by using more unusual varieties like opal basil, garlic chives, Italian parsley, and lemon thyme. Prepare the soil, add the plants, and fertilize according to the directions above.

Preparing Herb Planters

You can create many variations on the planter theme, following these general directions and then using the herbs and containers of your choice.

Begin by placing at least 2 inches of broken clay pots, sharp gravel, or other drainage material in the bottom of your container. Then fill it almost to the top with a basic potting soil mix. Scoop or dig out planting holes and set plants in place. Add soil to the top of the container, firming in plants well. Seeds of quick-growing annuals can be sown directly into containers—cover them with about ½ inch of soil, and press down lightly. Soak well with regular strength fish fertilizer. Drench the roots completely and fertilize steadily about once a week.

Edible Flower Planter

Plant List
1 calendula
1 chive
1 lavender
3 compact nasturtium, 3 trailing nasturtium
1 rose geranium
1 rectangular wooden planter box, 1 foot wide by 4 feet
    long by 8 inches deep

The renewed interest in cooking with flowers inspired this garden, which includes many of the best-tasting edible flowers. Grouped together in a rectangular wooden planter, they make a pretty sight and are easy to pick for the table.

Fill and fertilize your container according to the directions for preparing herb planters.

Create a row of calendula, chive, lavender, and rose geranium, spacing the plants equidistant from one another. The calendula and rose geranium are the quickest growing of these taller plants. Intersperse the nasturtiums between them, with the trailing ones nearest the edges. Place the nasturtiums in front. The annual calendula and nasturtiums will need to be replaced each season and the rose geranium moved indoors for the winter, but the other plants can remain in the planter year-round.

Italian Herb Planter Barrel

Plant List
2 sweet basil
1 sweet marjoram
1 Italian parsley
1 upright rosemary
1 thyme
1 oregano (optional)
1 half whiskey barrel (15 inches deep, 23 inches diameter)
24 qt. plastic packaging pellets

Nearly everyone loves the flavors of Italian herbs, and the five chosen for this easy garden are suitable for terra-cotta pots, window boxes, wooden half whiskey barrels, or even a sunny garden spot.

Add oregano to the list, by all means, but watch out for its spreading roots.

Fill the bottom of the half whiskey barrel 5 inches deep (⅓ full) with plastic packaging pellets. Add 2 cubic feet (about 28 dry quarts) of potting soil. Plant the herbs and fertilize according to the directions for preparing herb planters. When you set in the plants, remember that the basil and parsley will be the fastest growers. Give this barrel a sunny spot, and it will reward you with an abundance of flavorful herbs.

Herbes de Provence Planter

Plant List
2 basil
1 lavender (dwarf variety such as Munstead)
2 sweet marjoram
2 rosemary
1 summer savory
2 thyme

For a continental flavor, choose a weathered terra-cotta pot or a classically styled concrete planter that holds about five gallons. Fill the container with soil. Now plant with herbs of southern France. Center the lavender in the middle of the pot; arrange the other herbs around it in a pleasing pattern. Fertilize according to the directions for preparing herb planters.

Place this planter in full sun and watch the bees and butterflies enjoy it. The lavender, rosemary, and thyme are perennial; the others are annual.

Pacific Rim Planter

Plant List
1 sweet basil
1 Thai basil
1 packet cilantro seed
1 garlic chive
6 garlic plants
1 gingerroot or hot pepper plant (optional)
lemon grass (optional)
1 spearmint

The "Pacific Rim Planter" reflects the diverse populations of the maritime Northwest, incorporating plants of Japanese, Chinese, Vietnamese, and other Pacific Rim cultures. A lovely glazed pot from an Asian market or an old sake tub, if you have the good fortune to find one, would make a great container for this garden.

Fill a 5-gallon container according to the directions for preparing herb planters. Set the lemon grass and/or the hot pepper plant in the center, as they will grow tallest, and surround them with the other plants. Look at farmers' markets in late spring for already started garlic plants, which will mature with the other herbs. To keep the spearmint under control, you may wish to use a separate pot. Leave a 6-inch circle for the cilantro, and sow the seeds close together; make a second sowing in about a month for a continuous supply of leaves. Fertilize according to container planting directions earlier in this chapter.

If you find a sprouting gingerroot in the grocery store, tuck it in among the other plants. Hot peppers such as 'Super Cayenne' or 'Riot' are excellent container plants with lots of color. They keep producing until Christmas if brought into a cool greenhouse.

In this garden, cilantro, basil, and garlic are annuals, lemon grass is a tender perennial, and garlic chives and mint are perennials.

Kitchen Garden Plots

If you have the room and time to plant, consider creating a garden plot. Below are two gardens, of 16 and 24 square feet, respectively.

12-Herb Kitchen Garden

Plant List
6 sweet basil
2 chives
1 packet cilantro seed
1 packet dill seed
2 oregano
2 parsley
1 upright rosemary
1 sage
1 spearmint
1 tarragon
2 thyme
1 bay tree (optional)

All the herbs recommended in this book are suitable for a kitchen garden, but I consider the ones listed for the "12-Herb Kitchen Garden" to be the most basic. This pretty group would be perfect in a sunny area just outside the door. By the end of summer, it will be bursting with herbs, and by the following spring, you will have fairly sizable perennials and divisions of mint to give away. The bay tree is an extra that adds a charming focal point when sizable.

Make this garden 4 feet long on each side, nicely edged with bricks or stones. In mid-April, dig over the whole plot, working in 4 cubic feet of compost, to improve soil texture, and about 1 pound (2 cups) of all-purpose fertilizer. Rake it smooth enough for a seedbed.

Put your bay tree in the center, in a sunken pot or directly in the ground, remembering that you will probably take it indoors for the winter. Divide the remainder of the plot into four sections, each 4 square feet. Sow a 3-inch-wide band of cilantro around the perimeter of one bed, and one of dill around a second. About a month later, you can make a second sowing of these herbs around the remaining two beds. Save the center of the first square for six basil plants, to be set out in early May and protected from cold with plastic milk cartons (sans bottoms) until nights are warm. In the second square, plant one upright rosemary ('Arp' is hardiest), one sage, and two thyme plants. These three herbs have a similar tolerance for dry soil. In the third square, plant two chive plants, two parsley starts, and one tarragon. These herbs do best in a richer, moister soil. That leaves the fourth square for the spreaders, oregano and mint. Set the oregano nearest the bay tree, and either keep the mint in a pot and sink it into the ground or be prepared to keep slicing the roots with a shovel to keep it under control.

"Instant" 24-Herb Garden

Plant List
One of each: arugula, basil, bay, calendula, chives, cilantro, dill, fennel, garlic, lavender, lemon balm, lovage, marjoram, mint, nasturtium, oregano, parsley, rose geranium, rosemary, sage, savory, sweet cicely, tarragon, thyme

Janice and Joe Peltier of Herban Renewal in Seattle introduced me to a quick and easy way to make gardens. They successfully use their "No Till, Sheet Mulch Method" for many gardens around their urban lot. When a neighbor moved away and bequeathed me her compost heap, I tried this method for a wedge-shaped garden that came together in less than a day.

The varying heights of herbs in this garden make it a good candidate for a perennial border-type arrangement. When the plants are mature, the tall bay tree, fennel, and lovage dominate the background; at medium height are calendula, dill, scented geraniums, lavender, lemon balm, mint, oregano, rosemary, and sweet cicely; basil, sage, and savory fill in the middle; and low-growing chives, cilantro, garlic, nasturtium, parsley, tarragon, thyme, and winter savory are out in front.

This selection of herbs capitalizes on an interesting variety of leaf shapes and textures, flower colors, and fragrances. Annuals, including basil, calendula, cilantro, dill, nasturtiums, and summer savory, are interspersed with perennials and placed for easy access. As an added bonus, the flowers of many of these herbs attract bees to the garden: basil, cilantro, dill, lavender, lemon balm, lovage, marjoram, oregano, rosemary, summer savory, and thyme. Fennel is an important butterfly plant. Put the mint (sunk in pots to avoid invasiveness) and sweet cicely in a shady corner.

To plant, choose an area 4 feet wide by 6 feet long, perhaps along the south or west side of a fence or garage. Stake out the perimeter of the garden, and edge it with a sharp spade to kill grass roots. Dig out pernicious weeds such as dandelions and horsetail. Sprinkle a thin layer of compost or manure on the ground, and blanket it with two or three layers of flattened brown cardboard boxes, making sure the entire area is evenly covered (soak the boxes for easier handling). Then shovel on as much organic material as available: garden soil, worm castings, compost, kitchen waste, manure, shredded leaves. Build up mounds for varying heights of 1 to 3 feet if you like. Spread with 3 cups of all-purpose fertilizer and top it off with a thick layer of finished compost. Sow and plant your herbs directly into the bed and water them well. Within a very short time, your "instant" garden will fill in and look great.

Harvesting and Preserving

Summer has arrived, and your herbs are growing beautifully. Now what? Many people succeed in starting an herb garden but are at a loss when it comes to harvesting and storing what they have grown. Following are some general guidelines. Also check "Harvest and Preservation," under the individual herb listings in Chapter 5 for particulars.

HARVESTING

No set formula tells you when to cut herbs and how much to take, but the best time to harvest is just before a plant blooms, when the essential oils containing flavor and fragrance are at their peak. If you become impatient, start by cutting plants sparingly when they are 3 or 4 inches tall, and continue until they flower.

For most leafy herbs, cut the stems back to about 2 inches from the ground. With tougher-stemmed herbs like sage, snip or pinch off the leafy tops of the plant. "Pinching back" means using your thumbnails or clippers to remove plant tips, usually severing the stem just above a leaf node and taking less than a quarter of the plant's leaves. When harvesting fresh herbs for cooking or home remedies, you will probably cut only as much as needed right then. Snipping and clipping herbs regularly will keep them compact and productive.

If buds begin to form on an herb, harvest most of the plant and preserve it for winter. Afterward the plant will grow a second and sometimes a third crop.

If you do not cut your plants back, they will flower and go to seed; the leaves toughen and may turn yellow or brown. If it is not too late in the season, say mid-August, cut the plants back and wait for new growth; go ahead and use the leaves as long as they have good flavor and are not too tough. You may even be able to use the seedpods or flowers you have harvested.

After mid-September, slow down on harvesting perennials, since they are preparing for dormancy. If you cut too late in the season and stimulate new growth, your plants may not have the reserves needed to make it through a cold winter.

In short, do harvest and use your herbs. Nothing can compare to the flavors of herbs fresh from your garden.

PRESERVING AND STORING

Drying or freezing herbs and seeds for later use takes only a little time and effort. When the weather is dreadful, fresh herbs are few in your garden and expensive in the grocery store. The palette of flavors available from herbs you have grown can really brighten winter meals. One or more popular methods of preservation are right for each herb.

Drying Herbs

Herbs can be dried using a food dehydrator, a microwave, or air, depending upon time and availability. I do not recommend using an oven, except as specifically noted. General directions follow.

FOOD DEHYDRATOR: This time-saver produces dried herbs with great color and flavor. The usual dehydrator method is to chop the herbs, cutting out large fleshy midribs, or to strip the leaves from their stems, and then dry them at 90° to 110°F for 2 or 3 hours. Cool for a few minutes before testing for doneness—leaves should crumble in your hand.

MICROWAVE: Microwave ovens preserve the color and flavor of herbs beautifully, but can handle only about ¼ cup at a time. Place the herbs in a single layer between paper towels and microwave for 1 minute. Cool 1 minute and check. If they are not quite dry, try additional 30-second intervals.

AIR DRYING: The simplest way to preserve herbs, air drying usually takes two to three weeks. Bunch the herbs together with rubber bands, and hang them out of direct sunlight where air circulation is good until the leaves rustle between your fingers and feel brittle. As the stems dry and contract, the rubber bands shrink and hold them tight.

Tucked into a corner somewhere, the old-fashioned, collapsible wooden clothes-drying racks work well for herbs. If herbs take over your life, you may find yourself screwing hooks into the ceiling of an attic or utility room and stringing twine between them. This method is fine for many leafy herbs. When drying seeds used for flavoring, such as coriander, dill, and fennel, cut air holes in a paper bag and tie it around the stalks to catch seeds that drop off as they dry.

THE SIMPLE "NONMETHOD": By way of personal confession, one way I frequently air-dry herbs is the "lying around the kitchen" technique. Summers are busy here at my herb farm, and sometimes I do not get around to doing anything more with certain herbs than spreading them out on a paper plate or a sheet of paper. They blend in with the kitchen clutter until I finally get around to putting them in a jar. Small bunches of herbs also hang from utensil racks, cupboard hooks, and pushpins on the bulletin board until the winter day when I need a few sprigs of whatever for that night's dinner. When the next season's fresh herbs come along, the dried ones go in the compost. While I do not exactly recommend this nonmethod, the flavors of the herbs are still superior to most anything I could buy in a store.

For more information on preserving herbs, call your local county extension office.

Drying Seeds

Harvest ripe seeds from garden plants when they turn light brown, before they start dropping. Spread seed heads on screens or hang them in bunches over a cloth or inside a paper bag for about two weeks until dry. Rub off the dried seeds and store in an airtight container. Use this method to dry seeds for propagation as well as for cooking.

Herbs for Drying

Basil
Bay
Calendula (flowers)
Chives (flowers for ornament)
Dill (young leaves)
Fennel (stalks for stuffing
  baked fish, French-style;
  seed for seasoning)
Garlic
Lavender
Lemon Balm

Lovage
Marjoram
Mint
Oregano
Parsley
Rose Geranium
Rosemary
Sage
Savory
Tarragon
Thyme

Herbs for Freezing

Certain herbs better retain their flavor when frozen. The following herbs can last for six months in the freezer.

Basil (as pesto, or ground with olive oil)
Chives (leaves)
Cilantro (leaves)
Dill (chopped leaves or whole unripe seed heads)
Garlic (when cloves start to sprout)
Parsley (leaves)
Sweet Cicely (leaves)

STORING DRIED HERBS

Dried herbs last for one to two years when stored in appropriate airtight containers that protect them from heat, light, and moisture. Opaque glass or pottery jars and metal tins with tight-fitting lids are ideal. Be sure to label containers as you fill them. Do not use plastic; it breathes and allows the herbs to absorb moisture.

Whole leaves keep their flavors longer than ground or crumbled ones, but they also take up more room. To separate leaves from stems, rub a handful of herbs between your palms over a sheet of newspaper or old cloth. Compost the stems or use them for fire starters. Before storage, you may wish to chop the leaves coarsely in a food processor using a steel blade.

Freezing

The delicate flavors of certain herbs are better preserved by freezing than drying. Chives, cilantro, dill weed, and tarragon are among these, and I would not want to face a winter without a good supply of pesto made from my basil crop.

BLANCHING: This step is often recommended to stop enzyme action, which can compromise the flavor of frozen herbs. After gathering and lightly rinsing your herbs, dip them in boiling water for a few seconds; remove and plunge them in ice water. Drain the herbs on kitchen towels, then dry with a salad spinner or roll up in a dish towel.

Next, spread the herbs out on a cookie sheet and put them in the coldest part of your freezer, usually near the bottom. The leaves or pieces will freeze quickly and remain separate. Transfer your frozen herbs to a glass jar with a tight-fitting lid and return to the freezer.

HERB CUBES: Many people puree herbs with a little water, freeze them in ice-cube trays, and transfer the cubes to a glass jar. Use the premeasured herb cubes as needed to enhance your meals.

CHAPTER 5

Arugula to Thyme: 24 Herbs

This chapter describes in detail 24 herbs that will thrive in a maritime Northwest herb garden. About half of these are generally familiar; the rest are more unusual but worth planting. To narrow the list of herbs, I used three basic criteria: well-recognized culinary appeal, some ornamental value, and relative ease in growing. Several species and varieties are listed under some herbs. I have grown them all and recommend them for leaf or flower coloration and form, productivity, growth habit, scent, or other distinctive characteristics.

The selection encompasses herbs successful in various planting situations and growing conditions. Together, these herbs offer an array of flavors, colors, and textures for both your garden and your palate.

Arugula

Rocket, roquette, Italian cress. Cruciferae (Mustard or Cress family). *Eruca vesicaria* ssp. *sativa*.

DESCRIPTION: Arugula is a favorite Italian annual with dark green, deeply lobed leaves. Clusters of four-petaled white flowers are carried on 2- to 3-foot stems. Leaves and flowers have a nutty flavor, becoming

Quick Reference Guide

Find recipes for fertilizers and soil amendments in boxes on pages 5, 6, and 7 in Chapters 1 and 2. Organic pest and disease management also is detailed in Chapter 1. See Chapter 4 for information about harvesting and preserving herbs and seed saving. For sources of seeds, consult the Herb-Buying Directory, page 85.

more piquant as the plant grows older. The seeds are formed in pods at the top of the stalks, completing the entire life cycle of the plant in 3 to 4 months.

PROPAGATION AND CARE: Arugula flourishes in a rich, moist soil with partial shade or full sun. It is easy to grow, requiring only basic weeding and watering. Plants grown in the cool weather of spring and fall have the mildest flavor. Arugula is hardy enough to survive all but the coldest maritime Northwest winters.

Sow seeds directly where they are to grow; they germinate quickly. To maintain a continuous harvest, make your first sowing in mid-March and continue sowing every three weeks through September. If you space the plants 6 inches apart, they grow to the size of leaf lettuce. For European-style mesclun salads, sow thickly in rows or bands; within a few weeks you can cut handfuls of tender 3-inch leaves.

Because it is a heavy feeder, give this annual ample fertilizer and avoid planting it in the same place each season, although it reseeds freely.

PESTS AND DISEASES: Protect your arugula from flea beetles by placing a spun-bonded polyester row cover over it. Light and moisture can get in, but pests are kept out.

HARVEST AND PRESERVATION: When you cut back the plants for mesclun, drench them with regular solution fish fertilizer and more leaves will grow back quickly. You can harvest leaves of larger plants singly as needed, including the small ones growing on the flower stem. The flowers are edible too. When the plants are finished, pull them out and compost them.

IN THE KITCHEN: Arugula is best used fresh. Its distinctive flavor makes it a delicious substitute for lettuce in sandwiches and green salads, and adds a piquant accent to potato soups. Make a bed of arugula leaves and top with sliced bosc pears and goat cheese, or top with Bermuda onion rings and walnut-raspberry vinaigrette, garnished with arugula blossoms.

ORNAMENTAL USES: Arugula is a quick filler. Its green rosette makes an attractive addition to a kitchen garden and effectively contrasts with the grays of lavender and sage. It soon bolts and loses its compact form, but the cream-colored flowers stay on the plant for a long time.

Basil

Sweet basil. Labiatae (Mint family). *Ocimum basilicum*: 'Cinnamon', 'Dark Opal', Large Green, 'Citriodorum' (lemon),

'Crispum' (lettuce leaf), 'Purple Ruffles', 'Piccolo', 'Spicy Globe', 'Thai', and many more.

DESCRIPTION: Sweet basil, the most popular form of this aromatic herb, is a bushy annual that grows 2 to 3 feet tall. Its shiny, deep green leaves have smooth edges and grow in opposite pairs. The white flowers will attract bees to your garden.

The 'Crispum' variety has large, ruffled leaves and a more muted flavor than sweet basil. Both 'Dark Opal' and 'Purple Ruffles' have burgundy leaves and a good spicy taste. The flavor of 'Large Leaf' is milder, but its bigger leaves are good for wrapping foods. Lemon 'Citriodorum' basil grows to about 12 inches and has small, light green leaves with a fine lemony taste and scent. 'Piccolo' grows tall but with small leaves and excellent flavor. 'Spicy Globe' is a miniature with tiny leaves that forms a compact mound about 8 inches tall. The purplish leaves and stems of 'Cinnamon' and 'Thai' basil are sweeter and cinnamonlike.

PROPAGATION AND CARE: Give basil your sunniest spot. In tropical climates, it is a tall, luxuriant perennial. In the maritime Northwest, it takes all the sun it can get and will grow rapidly only during the height of summer. Cover transplants with spun-bonded polyester row covers to encourage quick growth. Technically, basil is hardy to 32°F, but it turns black at about 40°F, well before the first frost; treat it as a very tender annual.

All basils do best in a moderate to rich soil with steady, ample moisture. Work compost and organic fertilizers into the beds at planting time, then feed the plants regular fish fertilizer solution twice a month to sustain growth.

Some growers sow basil seed directly into the garden when the soil warms in late May. Since the herb takes about two months to mature, this makes for a short season if you plan to make pesto. For an earlier start, sow basil seeds indoors at two-week intervals beginning in mid-March. Seed germinates in 6 to 10 days at 60° to 70°F. A gel-like coating forms around the seeds once they are moistened, so keep them evenly watered to prevent hardening around the emerging shoots. Seedling leaves are rounded; true leaves are pointed and glossy.

Transplant the tiny seedlings to 2-inch pots and grow them until they have at least two sets of true leaves and are about 4 inches tall. Be sure to adapt the vulnerable starts to bright sunlight and night temperatures by hardening them off gradually. Wait until soil temperatures are 60°F at night before setting basil out. Try transplanting one batch of plants in mid-May, spacing them 8 to 10 inches apart, and a second batch two weeks later.

In mid-June, sow a few rows of seed directly into the garden for late-summer harvesting. Space direct-sown rows of basil about 2 feet apart, thinning the plants gradually (savor those thinnings!) to about 9 inches apart. To prolong your harvest, pot up plants from the garden and bring them indoors.

PESTS AND DISEASES: Slugs love basil as much as humans do, and they can mow down rows of seedlings overnight. Protect your plants using any of the methods described in "Organic Pest and Disease Management," in Chapter 1.

Flea beetles are also a problem. If the infestation is severe, dust the plants with rotenone on a still, dry morning. The tomato fruitworm can do tremendous damage even to large plants. Spraying with Thuricide has saved my basil crop from fruitworm.

HARVEST AND PRESERVATION: Your first picking of basil will probably be in mid- to late June. When the plants are 6 to 8 inches high and have four sets of leaves, pinch off the stems below the first two pairs of leaves. Two new stems, each with its own leaf pairs, will grow from the leaf node. Religiously pinch off those leafy tips and flower buds all season, and your plants will become bushy, abundant producers. Prevent basil from flowering or the stems will turn tough and woody with fewer and smaller leaves.

IN THE KITCHEN: Basil is one of the most popular cooking herbs. Pesto, with its multitude of uses, is practically synonymous with basil. Add basil to chicken dishes, to salmon and other fish, and to marinara sauce for pizza and pasta dishes. Lemon basil makes memorable fish and chicken as well as jellies and vinegars. Purple basils are great for colorful pesto and lovely in salads. 'Cinnamon' and 'Thai' basils add a wonderful spicy flavor to soups, sorbets, and teas.

ORNAMENTAL USES: Although all basils are handsome as ornamentals, certain varieties are particularly striking in the landscape. Bright green spheres of 'Spicy Globe', about 9 inches tall, make a beautiful edging for formal beds or along curving pathways. Colorful 'Opal' and 'Purple Ruffles' are dramatic accents when massed together or alternated with green basil, grayish sage, or lavender. Basil plants will quickly fill in spaces between slower-growing perennials.

Bay

Bay leaf, bay laurel, sweet bay. Lauraceae (Laurel family). *Laurus nobilis*: 'Aurea'.

DESCRIPTION: With its shiny, lance-shaped evergreen leaves and handsome form, a bay tree is an ornament in any herb garden. In its native Mediterranean climate, the bay tree is a hardy perennial that can reach 60 feet in height. In the maritime Northwest, it is half hardy, growing to 25 feet. With luck, pale yellow flowers will cover established bay trees in spring, but the decorative (and inedible) purple berries seldom ripen in this climate.

PROPAGATION AND CARE: Bay trees are often grown in pots set outside or sunk into the ground in summer and wintered indoors. Plant bay in a rich, well-drained soil mix, and feed potted trees occasionally with regular solution fish fertilizer or a slow-release commercial fertilizer. If you wish to grow yours outdoors, give it a very protected spot out of the wind. Cover the base of the plant with a heavy mulch of compost, leaf mold, or sawdust. Unless your location is exceptionally mild, you may have to wrap the tree with blankets to keep it from freezing in severe weather. I have lost so many beautiful bay trees to cold weather that I always bring them in.

Bay trees go dormant in the winter. A humid garage or cool greenhouse is the best place to keep them; mist the leaves often if you bring them into the house. When buds begin to swell along the stem, bring the plant into bright light and work some all-purpose fertilizer mix into the soil, about ¼ cup per gallon pot. Mist the leaves and water weekly. Set the tree outside in late March or April, fertilizing it once a month with ½ cup of regular solution fish fertilizer.

Notoriously difficult to propagate, bay trees can be started from seeds, cuttings, or suckers from established plants (seedlings look like miniature bay trees). Buying a young plant is easiest. Although slow-growing for the first two years, these trees reach a height of 4 feet and bush out within about four years. They can be trained into standards or topiary forms or allowed to grow naturally.

There is no need to prune your bay until it becomes fairly large. Then just trim branches above leaf nodes as necessary during the growing season to achieve a nicely shaped plant.

PESTS AND DISEASES: Watch out for disk-shaped scale insects. In their final, egg-laying stage of life, these creatures attach themselves to the stems and undersides of leaves and suck nourishment from them. Scale insects produce a sticky honeydew attractive to ants, which carry the infestation to other plants. Honeydew also encourages the growth of black, sooty molds that can slow photosynthesis. Scrape off scale by hand, or spray plants with a "superior" dormant oil before leaf buds open. **HARVEST AND PRESERVATION:** Harvest bay leaves from the tree year-round and use them fresh or dried. To dry leaves flat, press them in a book.

IN THE KITCHEN: The aromatic qualities of bay leaves are valued for classic scents including Windsor, bay rum, or a combination of bay, rose, and lavender. In cooking, add the flavorful leaves to soups, stews, meat dishes, pickled meats and vegetables, and sauces. Rub the leaves firmly with the back of a spoon to release the flavor before using.

ORNAMENTAL USES: Bay trees have long been popular as the focal points of herb gardens, often in the center of a round garden or as twin pillars along a path. Evergreen foliage gives even small bay trees an elegant look that enhances formal and informal gardens alike. The pale yellow spring flowers are delightful. Bay tree topiaries in decorative pots are often set on the steps of London homes and shops, a custom maritime Northwest city dwellers might well adopt.

Calendula

Pot marigold, garden marigold. Compositae (Sunflower or Daisy family). *Calendula officinalis*: 'Bon Bon', 'Kablouna', 'Lemon Coronet', 'Pacific Brights', and others.

DESCRIPTION: Calendula, the old-fashioned marigold, is considered a hardy annual, but it survives only our mildest winters unless protected from hard frost.

The 4-inch-long green leaves with rounded ends grow sparsely on thick, fleshy stems. Bright orange or yellow daisylike blossoms with dark brown centers bloom atop the stems throughout the summer, although they tend to flag somewhat in hot weather. As a child I was fascinated by the unusual and varied seeds, some curving and sharply ridged, others small and smooth.

In addition to cooking, this versatile herb is used for fresh bouquets, potpourri, and medicines. The old-fashioned species grows to about 2 feet and can become straggly, but is preferred for medicinal uses. Calendula heals and rejuvenates the skin, and is used in lotions, salves, and soaps for babies and adults.

PROPAGATION AND CARE: Give calendula moderately rich soil and moisture, and plant it in full sun for best results.

Sow seed indoors in February or March, or outdoors March through June. Overwintered seed from outdoor autumn sowing also does well; calendula reseeds freely, often popping up as soon as the cold weather ends. Seedlings have pairs of 2-inch narrow leaves, tapering towards the stem. Keep the flowers picked and remove seed heads to prolong blooming. If flower production dwindles, try cutting plants back severely; before long they should look better than ever.

PESTS AND DISEASES: Sometimes you will find the petals of calendula blossoms chewed, but usually the damage is limited to a few flowers. Examine flower heads carefully for tiny insects, which can be washed off.

HARVEST AND PRESERVATION: Cut calendula when the flowers have opened fully, preferably in late morning when they are free of dew. Immediately place cut stems for bouquets in warm water. For culinary or medicinal use, pick only the heads; dry them on screens in a warm place or in a dehydrator.

IN THE KITCHEN: Use the fresh flowers whole as a garnish, or sprinkle the colorful petals on salads, desserts, and entrées. Fresh or dried, calendula is reminiscent of saffron in egg, cheese, and rice dishes.

ORNAMENTAL USES: New calendula varieties have bushy growth and special flower characteristics and colors. 'Bon Bon' is an early 10-inch dwarf variety that comes in orange, yellow, or apricot. 'Lemon Coronet', a dense, erect plant, has fully double yellow flowers. The dense, crested blossoms of 'Kablouna' feature short quills in yellow, gold, and orange and make lovely bouquets. The 'Pacific Giant Mix' has semidouble flowers in shades of cream, yellow, apricot, and orange. Dried whole, the flower heads brighten potpourris and are especially suitable with citrus mixtures.

Chives

Chives. Liliaceae (Lily family). *Allium schoenoprasum* (common): 'Forsgate' or 'Forescate', 'Grolau'; *A. tuberosum* (garlic chives).

DESCRIPTION: The versatile onion flavor, easy care, neat appearance, and compact growth habit of chives place it among the top favorites of herb gardeners. A perennial, it grows in a clump, like miniature green onions, with deep green, tubular leaves a foot high, crowned with globular, pink, edible flowers in the spring. Of the few named varieties, 'Forsgate' is a vigorous grower with showy flowers, and 'Grolau' is particularly suitable for forcing indoors in winter. Less well known is a close relative, garlic chives, which have flat leaves, starry white, edible blossoms, and a sweet flavor that hints of garlic.

PROPAGATION AND CARE: Chives do best in full sun to partial shade in a moist soil rich in organic matter. Amend the soil with rotted manure or compost before planting. Weed the plants well as they become established, taking care to keep grasses out. The roots of some grasses look just like chive roots and are difficult to remove—if even a small piece remains, the grass will grow back.

Thickly sow seeds of either kind of chives in a seed tray or flat in March (indoors) or April (outdoors). Once the grasslike seedlings are about 3 inches high and have developed sturdy roots, take a sharp knife and cut into 2-inch squares, as you would a cake. Each of these squares will become a plant. Tuck them in the ground, and within a few months they can be harvested. When the plants are 3 years old, dig them up in spring or fall and divide each one into four plants. It does not take long to grow a big chive patch!

Once the plants bloom, the leaves begin to shrivel and turn yellow, so harvest them steadily to forestall flowering. In late fall, the entire plant will die back. This is a fine time to generously mulch your plants with compost or manure to get them off to a flying start in spring.

PESTS AND DISEASES: Insect problems with chives are minimal. Watch for aphids on new starts. Although uncommon, the most serious problem is rust, a fungus that appears as orange spots on the leaves. Dig and burn affected plants, and start over with healthy plants in a different location.

HARVEST AND PRESERVATION: Cut chives from the bottom, about 2 inches from the ground, to stimulate new growth. Remove tough flower stems. You can dry chives in the microwave or in the dehydrator at a low heat, but freezing preserves the flavor and texture better. Chop and spread chives on cookie sheets according to directions under "Freezing" in Chapter 4. Chive flowers hold their shape and color when dried for everlasting wreaths and bouquets. Harvest the flowers by hand or with scissors, reaching down to the bottom of the stem, and hang to air-dry.

IN THE KITCHEN: Chopped chives have myriad uses in the kitchen— for salads, dips, and dressings, topping baked potatoes and hot or cold soups, and more. Garlic chives, cut in inch-long pieces, are delicious in stir-fries and can give salads an Asian twist. The flowers have an intense onion flavor and are beautiful garnishes for salads, soups, and entrées.

ORNAMENTAL USES: In the landscape, chives make charming edging plants along paths. Try planting them with lower-growing herbs like thyme or 'Spicy Globe' basil, with a background screen of taller calendula, mature sages and lavenders, or scented geraniums. The reedlike form of chives is an interesting counterpoint to the textures of Italian parsley, nasturtium, or rosemary. Although they die back in winter, chives provide early color when their pink flowers bloom in early spring.

Cilantro

Chinese parsley, Mexican parsley, coriander (seeds). Umbelliferae (Carrot family). *Coriandrum sativum* (common): 'Slowbolt', 'Santo'.

DESCRIPTION: A penetrating odor and equally strong flavor characterize cilantro, which has flat, rounded leaves with serrated edges resembling Italian parsley. Mature plants are 1 to 4 feet tall, depending on growing conditions, with a single taproot. Seed stalks, which have feathery leaves, form quickly, topped by umbels of edible, pinkish white flowers.

Round, striated seeds (technically fruits) of ⅛ inch ripen from green to brown. Known as coriander, the seeds have a warm, spicy flavor quite different from the leaves.

For years, this annual was bred to bolt and quickly produce coriander seed. Since the leaves are now considered desirable, slow-bolting strains are becoming available.

PROPAGATION AND CARE: Ideal conditions for growing cilantro include a sunny location, a well-fertilized soil with good drainage, and steady watering. For best results, sow coriander seed about ½ inch deep, directly where it is to grow. Keep the soil moist until germination occurs, usually in two to three weeks. Seedling leaves are narrow and elongated. If you transplant young cilantro plants, be very gentle with the taproots.

Thickly sown bands of cilantro, about 4 inches wide, are productive and easy to harvest. Single rows waste garden space, and broadcasting seeds results in beds that are exasperating to weed. In pots or planter boxes, sow clusters of seeds.

Begin sowing in March or early April and continue at three-week intervals for a continuous supply of fresh leaves. Keep the plants weeded, especially when they are small. They will tolerate light frost, and by using spun-bonded polyester row covers, you can extend the season by two to four weeks. Cilantro reseeds freely.

PESTS AND DISEASES: Slugs and insects steer clear of cilantro, and I have had no disease problems.

HARVEST AND PRESERVATION: Harvest when plants are 3 to 6 inches tall. Pull them out by the roots, or use the "cut and come again" method: grasp a handful of plants and cut them back to the ground. Drench the remaining stalks with a light fish fertilizer solution, keep well watered, and the plants will come back again. You can repeat this process four or five times a season as the plants reach harvestable size.

Although powerful, the flavor of fresh cilantro is not easily preserved. When I have no fresh cilantro, I buy it at the grocery store. Dried cilantro is hardly worth using. I do freeze the leaves, however, as pesto or in salsa. Try freezing leaves, using the methods described in "Freezing," Chapter 4, to see if you agree with me.

IN THE KITCHEN: Cilantro's exuberant flavor is appreciated in many parts of the world. It is a must in salsa, enchiladas, ceviche, and other Mexican specialties; Vietnamese chicken soup and Thai mushroom soup; and East Indian chutneys. Add a few leaves to chicken, crab, and Asian salads. Use the seeds in curries and breads, and for pickling cucumbers and meats. Roots are used extensively in Thai cooking.

ORNAMENTAL USES: The quick life cycle of cilantro prevents it from being a standout. The attractive, deep green leaves of compact young plants add texture to container plantings, and the delicate laciness of the pinkish white flowers will fill in gaps in the garden, but the effect in both cases is short-lived.

Dill

Dill. Umbelliferae (Carrot family). *Anethum graveolens*: 'Bouquet', Dukat, 'Fernleaf', 'Long Island Mammoth', 'Tetra', and others.

DESCRIPTION: Dill is an attractive annual herb with feathery green leaves and umbels of tiny yellow flowers. It grows from a single taproot, reaching 18 inches to 4 feet. The ripe seed—brown, ribbed, and flat— is ready to harvest about three months after the plant first germinates.

Common, 'Long Island Mammoth', and 'Bouquet' are tall varieties that produce large umbels of green seed for pickling. 'Dukat', 'Tetra', and 'Fernleaf' are extra-leafy dwarf types grown for fresh-cut dill weed or baby dill leaves. They are good choices for growing in containers.

PROPAGATION AND CARE: Choose a sunny location out of the wind with moderate to rich soil. About all it takes for success is to keep young plants weeded and watered.

Sow dill seed directly where it is to grow (or transplant carefully). I scatter the seed thickly in bands 4 inches wide, which results in nice stands of baby dill that are much easier to weed and harvest than broadcasted seed. Seed germinates in 7 to 21 days. Two long, narrow seedling leaves are followed by feathery true leaves.

If pickling dill is your objective, timing your planting to be ready when cucumbers are ripe can be a gamble. The best insurance is to keep sowing every three weeks from late March or early April through June. Keep harvesting baby dill, leaving some plants from each sowing to mature, and you will get it right. For extended harvests of baby dill, make sowings through late August and blanket them with spun-bonded polyester row covers as the weather cools. Late plantings can survive light frosts. Dill reseeds abundantly in the garden.

PESTS AND DISEASES: In my experience, aphids are the only insects to attack dill. If the problem is not severe, simply wash the cut dill well before using it; otherwise, insecticidal soap is a good organic control.

HARVEST AND PRESERVATION: To harvest baby dill, cut the entire plant to the ground using scissors or clippers. If the plants are in bands, you can cut a handful with one snip. Drench the cut row with regular fish fertilizer solution, keep it watered, and within weeks a second cutting will be ready. Or allow a few plants, spaced 6 to 8 inches apart, to grow until mature. For pickling dill, cut seed heads when they are large, green, and plump. Harvest ripe seed heads for seasoning or propagating when they flatten and turn brown and the stems are drying out.

My favorite way to preserve dill is to lay the green seed heads out on a baking sheet, freeze them, then rub the seeds off and transfer them to glass jars. They taste great and are easy to use in any recipe that calls for fresh dill. Alternatively, dry chopped dill leaves in a dehydrator for bright green dill weed, or freeze chopped leaves.

IN THE KITCHEN: Dill is one of the most widely used herbs. Fresh baby dill (or dried dill weed), green seed (or pickling dill), and ripe dill seed all have distinct flavors. Baby dill and dill weed are the most delicate; both are popular with fish, cucumbers, and tea breads. In Scandinavia, baby dill traditionally flavors gravlax and new potatoes. Try it with beets, green beans, carrots, peas, and potato salads. Pickling dill enhances pickled green beans and asparagus as well as cucumbers. Dill seed is used in pickling spice mixtures, mustards, and breads.

ORNAMENTAL USES: As an annual, dill has only a temporary place in the garden, yet its feathery green color, strong vertical lines, and shapely seed heads are very ornamental. Consider it as a backdrop for other plants in a border, for adding height to groupings in planters, or as a quick-growing foliage plant with an excellent filling or softening effect.

Fennel

Fennel. Umbelliferae (Carrot family). *Foeniculum vulgare*: var. *rubra* (copper or bronze), var. *azoricum* (Florence).

DESCRIPTION: With its feathery green leaves and branched seed heads, common fennel looks like oversized dill. Although they are related, fennel is a hardy perennial that is easily distinguished from dill by the sweet licorice flavor present in all parts of the plant.

Fennel grows from a large, white taproot, which increases in size by producing offsets. Finely cut leaves unfold gradually from sheaths, which can reach 2 feet in length. Glossy and bright in spring, the leaves lose their shine and become dark over the season. Stems are succulent when young and become hollow with age. A seed stalk gradually rises up to 8 feet from the middle of the plant and produces umbels of small yellow flowers attractive to bees. Ripe seeds are ⅛ inch long, oval, and greenish gray. In the coldest areas of the maritime Northwest or in deep shade, seeds ripen poorly. Fennel plants die back to the ground in winter but reappear in early spring and can live for many years.

Copper or bronze fennel is slightly more frost tolerant than common fennel and has rich, darkly colored leaves. Florence fennel or finoccio, an annual relative grown for the tasty bulbous base of its stems, requires a long, warm growing season.

PROPAGATION AND CARE: A tough survivor, fennel is often found growing along roadsides or in vacant lots. Given enough sun, it will grow almost anywhere but does best in a fertile, fairly moist yet well-drained soil. The plants are completely hardy in the maritime Northwest climate.

Start fennel from small plants, from seed sown in spring or fall, or from root divisions. This herb reseeds freely, and the tiny seedlings, which first appear with two long, narrow leaves, quickly grow to sizable plants. Divide the roots every three years in early spring or fall.

Fertilizer is seldom needed. To keep plants producing tender leaves, cut them back to the ground when they begin going to seed and water them well once or twice a week.

To prevent an overabundance of fennel plants in your garden, harvest *all* the seeds. Then cut back woody stems to the ground for a neat winter appearance. Winter protection is unnecessary, but be sure the roots are not in standing water. If your clumps of fennel are growing too large, the best time to dig them out is in early spring or late fall.

PESTS AND DISEASES: Aphids are fond of fennel, especially copper fennel. Sometimes thorough washing before using the leaves is enough to remove bugs, but, if not, insecticidal soap spray is an efficient control.

HARVEST AND PRESERVATION: Young fennel leaves are most tender and delicious—pick them fresh throughout the season. Seeds ripen unevenly, a few heads at a time. Cut heads of green seeds and dry them upside down in bunches for later use in herb wreaths and everlasting bouquets. Harvest ripe seeds when they turn light brown, before they start dropping.

IN THE KITCHEN: Fennel is valuable for cooking and medicine. Its leaves add a sweet licorice flavor to salads and are traditionally used with poached or baked fish. The seeds, with a stronger flavor and sweet aftertaste, perk up Italian sausage, spaghetti sauce, and fruit salads. In India, fennel seeds are served candied or toasted as an after-dinner treat. Nibble them straight from the garden to aid digestion while freshening the breath. They are often added to cough syrups for their soothing, mildly expectorant effect.

ORNAMENTAL USES: Although it grows large, fennel makes a handsome backdrop in a perennial border or herb garden. Also use it for screening effects. Children love the licorice flavor, so plant it near their play areas or in their own gardens. Ornamentally, copper fennel, with its burnished leaves, makes a dramatic contrast to gray plants such as dusty miller, silver king artemisia, cardoon, globe thistle, and artichoke, or white flowers such as Florentine iris (orris root plant). Copper fennel is also luscious with pale pink, white, or apricot roses, and it blends beautifully with like-colored plants: opal basil, shiso or beefsteak herb, bearded iris, and Japanese maples.

Garlic

Garlic. Liliaceae (Lily family). *Allium sativum*: 'California Early', 'Silverskin', 'Italian Purple', 'Spanish Roja', 'Korean Red', and others; *A. ampeloprasum* (elephant garlic).

DESCRIPTION: Garlic is a perennial bulb, like lilies or tulips, to which it is related. A single clove develops into a head or bulb of 4 to 15 cloves. Roots sprout from the plump end of the clove; four or more long, flat leaves with lengthwise ribs grow from the pointed end. A flower stem may form, topped by a globe of florets which produces angular black seeds. In other varieties, clovelike bulbils form atop the stems. New cloves form at the base of the leaves, encased in a thin white or reddish sheath or skin.

Garlic falls into two categories—hard-neck and soft-neck—of which there are many types with various flavors, sizes, and keeping qualities. Soft-neck varieties can be braided; hard-neck types form tough, unwieldy stems. Popular soft-neck varieties include 'California Early', 'Silverskin', and 'Italian Purple'. Hard-neck varieties include 'Spanish Roja' and 'Korean Red'. Elephant garlic, a different species, is gigantic, mild flavored, and a superlative keeper.

PROPAGATION AND CARE: Garlic needs full sun and well-drained soil with plenty of nutrients. It takes several months to mature, but not much space; you can tuck it in among your flowers and vegetables. Prepare the planting area by digging in compost, aged manure, or other organic material, plus all-purpose fertilizer mix.

Garlic is most commonly propagated from cloves. Although the bulbs grow biggest when planted from October through December, planting can be done as late as March. Garlic will not freeze out in the maritime Northwest, but it can rot with poor drainage. Young plants are often available in the spring at nurseries and farmers' markets.

Plant the cloves plump-side down, about 1 inch deep and 4 inches apart. Mulch the entire planting with a 4- to 6-inch layer of straw or alfalfa hay to keep weeds down. For container gardening, follow the same general directions, omitting the mulch.

Beginning in May, water the garlic to keep it from drying out. Pull or hoe weeds and keep applying mulch. In mid- to late July, when the leaf tips first begin to turn yellow, quit watering or problems with diseases and split skins may develop.

PESTS AND DISEASES: Garlic is so distasteful to aphids, cabbage moths, slugs, and other pests that preparations made from it have long been used as insect repellents.

Garlic is vulnerable to mold and fungus diseases. Gray or botrytis mold appears at harvest time if plants are watered too much late in the season or if the garlic tops are cut before proper curing (see "Harvest and Preservation" below). Infection begins with a leaf blight and moves into the neck of the bulb (which looks water-soaked), and then gray mold turns the neck black, destroying the entire bulb—not a pretty sight. To prevent gray mold, avoid overwatering late in the season and cure the bulbs well.

Another serious disease, white rot, has ravaged garlic plantings in recent years. The leaves of diseased plants decay at the base, turn yellow, and topple over. Gray or blackish filaments of rot appear in the neck and bulb, roots rot, and the plant can be pulled up easily. Destroy all diseased cloves and avoid planting garlic or any alliums in the affected areas for up to 10 years. To prevent this disease from getting your garlic, grow only certified stock.

Your local county cooperative extension agent can help you identify garlic diseases.

HARVEST AND PRESERVATION: When stalks start to wither and plants turn brown, your garlic is ready to harvest. Dig it with a garden fork or spade on a dry day, being careful not to injure the bulbs. Remove dirt from around the bulb by rubbing it off or stripping off the outer leaves down to the base.

Dry heads in a warm, shady, nonhumid garage or shed until the cloves feel hard and their skins are papery. Bunch or braid them when the leaves are still pliant but dry enough not to mold, or simply remove the tops and store the heads in a mesh bag in a cool, dry area with good air circulation. When cloves begin to sprout in spring, you can peel and freeze them in glass jars with tight lids.

IN THE KITCHEN: Volumes have been written on the gustatory pleasures of garlic, and festivals have been dedicated to the enjoyment of this herb. Its uses in the kitchen are endless. Raw, garlic is almost mandatory in salads, whether a clove is discreetly rubbed on the serving bowl or flagrantly added to herb vinegars and salad dressings. Because its flavor mellows when cooked, garlic enhances almost any savory dish. It is sumptuous baked and spread on crusty French bread.

Garlic also has well-documented medicinal value. It is known to fight bacterial and viral infections, help reduce high blood pressure and triglyceride levels, and aid digestion.

ORNAMENTAL USES: Though seldom regarded as ornamentals, culinary garlics can add interesting vertical lines to a planting. Rows of garlic in my gardens have even been mistaken for daffodils. The wide leaves of elephant garlic, while not showy in a conventional sense, are quite dramatic when massed. Elephant garlic's globular flower heads are attractive, while the stems of 'Korean Red' have unusual twisting lines. Garlic is often planted near roses to improve their scent and to repel aphids.

Lavender

Lavender. Labiatae (Mint family). *Lavandula angustifolia* (vera or English lavender): 'Munstead', 'Nana Alba', 'Jean Davis', 'Hidcote'; *L. latifolia* (spike); *L.* × *intermedia* (lavandin): 'Grosso', 'Seal', 'Provence'; *L. dentata* (French or fringed); *L. stoechas* (Spanish): 'Otto Quast'.

DESCRIPTION: Lavender is an herb that has it all. This perennial evergreen shrub with gray-green leaves is crowned in summer with spikes of fragrant purple blossoms. The plants grow from 1 to 3 feet high, depending on variety, to which the flower spikes add another foot or two.

There are several species of lavender, and many more named varieties of each, which sometimes leads to confusion. Angustifolia varieties are "basic" lavenders: familiar, hardy, fragrant, and easy to grow. They produce top-quality essential oil. 'Vera' or 'English' is very hardy and reaches 3 feet, with lavender blossoms on 2-foot stems. 'Hidcote' is a handsome 2-foot-high lavender with deep purple flowers. 'Jean Davis', about 2½ feet tall, has pale pink flowers. 'Munstead' is the smallest, only about 1½ feet high, and has deep purple blossoms on short stems.

L. latifolia (spike lavender) is grown in the Mediterranean region for its relatively inexpensive essential oil. *L. dentata* (French) and *L. stoechas* (Spanish) are distinctive species, with toothed leaves and plump flowers. 'Otto Quast' is sometimes sold as 'Rabbit Ear' lavender. Lovely in the garden but intolerant of frost, it is less fragrant than other varieties. The × *intermedia* or lavandin varieties are created by crossing *L. angustifolia* with *L. latifolia* to produce large, beautiful, fragrant, and hardy plants, which bloom continuously through the summer. 'Grosso', 'Seal', and 'Provence' are lavandins grown commercially for their essential oil.

PROPAGATION AND CARE: Select a sunny location with average to poor well-drained soil. Lavender is extremely tolerant of heat and drought, but it cannot survive wet soils in winter.

Except for lavandin hybrids, lavender can be started from seed, but germination can be difficult and not all plants will be uniform. For best results, sow fresh seed indoors in spring or fall, keeping the soil temperature at 75° to 80°F. Seedlings are often grayish in color, with stiff leaves that smell like lavender. Cuttings of all species taken in spring and fall root easily, though they grow slowly the first year.

Lavender plants require minimal maintenance. Fertilizing is

optional, but 2 tablespoons of lime can be scratched into the soil around the roots each spring to good effect. Cut back all the spent bloom stalks in autumn. Dig tender varieties as frost approaches and pot them up to winter in a sheltered place. Cut plants back by at least half in January or February, and set them out in the garden only after all danger of frost has passed.

After about five years, the stems of English lavenders become tough and woody. I have never been brave enough to cut such plants back to the ground in hopes that they would rejuvenate as some have advised. I *have* replanted them, however, burying the stems with considerable effort and unimpressive results.

PESTS AND DISEASES: Lavender usually remains clean of insect pests and does not seem susceptible to disease. A few brown, withered leaves at the base of the stems is normal and does not indicate a problem.

HARVEST AND PRESERVATION: For decorative bundles of lavender to hang up or give as gifts, harvest lavender while the buds are closed; opened flowers shatter when dried. Lavender destined for culinary uses and potpourri can be harvested in midbloom. When making lavender wands—old-fashioned woven sachets—cut long flower stems while they're in full bloom.

IN THE KITCHEN: The marvelous, clean fragrance of lavender, its stellar attribute, is an asset in cooking and teas. A few fresh flower pips add a piquant flavor to Greek salads. Combine the dried flowers with basil, fennel seed, savory, and thyme for a versatile herbes de Provence seasoning, good with lamb or cottage cheese. Try a lavender ice for a refreshing summer treat.

ORNAMENTAL USES: The varying colors and heights of lavender are a beautiful sight massed together. Its soft grayish foliage looks good year-around, providing a sense of repose in a garden of silver and gray shades, and offers a handsome backdrop for brighter colors. Lavender's neat, rounded shapes create undulating curves that can carry the viewer's eye with quiet motion or direct it to a focal point. Dwarf lavenders are often planted with roses to create a fragrant and romantic atmosphere. Lavenders also make beautiful edging plants, releasing their scent as passersby brush against the leaves. Shorter varieties can define a path yet allow views of plants farther into the garden, and taller varieties can serve a dual purpose as edging and screen or garden room divider. Also use these plants in potpourris, sachets, and toiletries of all kinds.

Top: Copper fennel provides a soft counterpoint to bright flowers. **Center left:** Chives with creeping golden marjoram. **Center right:** Vivid nasturtiums brighten the garden; lovage leaves in the background. **Bottom:** Summer's bounty: dill flower, 'Piccolo' and 'Dark Opal' sweet basil, nasturtium, anise hyssop, and cilantro.

Top: Fennel adds height and drama to a perennial border. Note the bright yellow blossoms. **Center left:** Pale pink flowers of summer savory with feathery dill leaves, green dill seed, curled and Italian parsley. **Center right:** Colorful foliage of 'Golden' sage, 'Tricolor' sage, and creeping golden marjoram. **Bottom:** Evergreen and perennial, mature rosemary provides a mass of bloom in the spring. Irrepressible mint is popping up at left.

Top left: A harvest of garlic.
Top right: Sage in full bloom
with angelica in background.
In this setting, these common
herbs are surprisingly handsome. **Center left:**
Variegated lemon thyme
neatly edges a planting of
lettuce. **Bottom:** Rugged,
dependable, fragrant, and
glorious in bloom—lavender
is a real garden asset.

Top: The delicate beauty of silver thyme and 'The Fairy' rose make a felicitous combination. **Right:** Easy-care sweet cicely has elegant foliage and fragrant blossoms. **Bottom left:** Variegated lemon balm (*Melissa officinalis* 'Aurea') is a colorful variation on the familiar garden standby. **Bottom right:** Golden calendula and orange nasturtium flowers can accent a meal as well as a garden.

Lemon Balm

Sweet balm, common balm. Labiatae (Mint family). *Melissa officinalis*: 'Golden' or 'Aurea', 'Variegata', 'Lime'.

DESCRIPTION: Lemon balm is an herbaceous perennial with square, downy stems, which grows from a fibrous root system to about 2½ feet. Its soft, rounded, crinkly leaves are 2 to 3 inches long, notched at the edges, with a musky lemon flavor and aroma. Leaves of the common variety are light green; variegated lemon balm has splashes of gold, while leaves of 'Aurea' are golden. Lime balm, a near relative, has a similar appearance but a less musky citrus scent.

The plants die down in winter but are up again in very early spring. Inconspicuous white flowers bloom in clusters at the leaf axils, producing tear-shaped, light brown seeds of about ⅟₁₆ inch. Lemon balm increases in size gradually and does not spread rampantly like mints.

PROPAGATION AND CARE: I first discovered this herb growing vigorously alongside an old barn, the last evidence of a long-abandoned garden. At my farm, lemon balm grows in a sunny bed, under our plant benches in heavy shade, and even from cracks in the sidewalk. Still, it is not a pernicious weed, just a nice plant to have around.

Although it does best in rich, moist soil and partial shade, lemon balm will also grow in dry soils. Once established, it is among the easiest herbs to grow. Maintenance is optional, but to keep plants looking neat you might whack them down once or twice in summer. Lemon balm is so hardy in the Pacific Northwest (to 0°F) that there is no need to mulch it for the winter, but its roots will rot in standing water.

Seeds germinate readily under glass in spring or broadcast in the garden in spring or fall. Their smooth, rounded first leaves give way to crinkly true leaves. Plants can be divided in any season, but they reseed so freely that it is seldom necessary to assist in increasing their numbers.

PESTS AND DISEASES: Garden webworms cause some leaf curl, which can be alleviated with Thuricide.

HARVEST AND PRESERVATION: A vigorous lemon balm will yield up to three harvests each season. Cut the stems off near the base before the plants bloom. The delicate flavor is best when the herb is fresh, but the dried herb is useful for teas and potpourri. Hang small bunches to dry in a warm, airy place until brittle, or dry in a dehydrator. Then strip the dried leaves and store in airtight containers.

IN THE KITCHEN: Lemon balm adds a fresh taste to green salads, fruit cups, and sorbets. Try it in stuffings for lamb, pork, or chicken, or in homemade mayonnaise with fish. It is also excellent in teas, alone or combined with fresh-squeezed lemons and frozen lemonade. Or the cook may want to pour a quart of boiling water over a large bunch of fresh (or 1 cup dried) lemon balm, steep for 10 minutes, and strain into a soothing herbal bath for stress relief.

ORNAMENTAL USES: Golden variegated lemon balm is lovely in informal gardens, especially in the shade combined with the chartreuse of lady's mantle or contrasting deep greens. Lemon balm is also a pleasant addition to a tea garden. In a tussie mussie garden, where plants are grown in various combinations for their symbolic values, lemon balm represents sympathy.

Lovage

Lovage, love parsley, sea parsley. Umbelliferae (Carrot family). *Levisticum officinale*.

DESCRIPTION: A big, robust perennial, lovage has thick, fleshy roots and large, deeply lobed leaves, which grow on hollow stalks 2 to 3 feet long. From the center of the plant a thick flower stalk rises 4 to 7 feet, crowned with an umbel of inconspicuous, sticky chartreuse flowers attractive to bees. The seeds are flat, ridged ovals.

PROPAGATION AND CARE: Lovage is tough and adaptable, growing lushly in a rich, moist soil with full sun or partial shade and less vigorously in poor soil. Completely hardy in the maritime Northwest, it will come up year after year.

Lovage is easily grown from seeds, best sown when freshly collected in late summer. It also can be propagated from offsets sliced from the roots in early spring. Lovage requires no special care other than reasonable weeding. In a moist spot, it will need no watering. When unharvested leaves turn yellow, cut back the whole plant to encourage new growth. Remove the leaves and seed stalk when the plant dies down to keep the garden tidy.

PESTS AND DISEASES: Lovage usually is not bothered by pests or disease.

HARVEST AND PRESERVATION: Harvest lovage leaves and stems by cutting them back to the base of the plant. Remove the thick stems, cut out fleshy midribs, then dry the leaves in a dehydrator or a very low oven below 150°F.

IN THE KITCHEN: The strong, intriguing flavor of lovage is reminiscent of celery with hints of allspice. In Europe it is a favorite for soups, stews, roasts, and savory dishes. Maggi, the Swiss seasoning concentrate, has a lovage flavor. Try grilling salmon with lovage butter, or adding a few fresh leaves to a green or tuna salad. Simmer stalks in tomato juice. The hollow stems make great "lovage straws" for sipping tomato juice or Bloody Marys on lazy summer afternoons. Roots and seeds are also edible but are rarely utilized.

ORNAMENTAL USES: Although the tall chartreuse flowers attract bees, they are inconspicuous. Leaves are a beautiful deep green, however. Because of its height and shade tolerance, lovage befits the back of a border where you need something big and bold.

Marjoram

Sweet marjoram, knotted marjoram. Labiatae (Mint family). *Origanum marjorana.*

DESCRIPTION: One of the most exquisitely aromatic of culinary herbs, sweet marjoram is an 8- to 12-inch plant with ¼- to 1-inch soft, oval, opposite leaves and branching stems. It is easily distinguished from oregano and other relatives by the unusual ball or knotlike clusters of tiny white flowers at the top of the stems. Although sweet marjoram is a tender perennial that can be wintered over indoors, it is usually grown as an annual in the maritime Northwest.

PROPAGATION AND CARE: Like basil, sweet marjoram prefers sunshine and warm temperatures. It needs rich soil with added compost or all-purpose fertilizer. Sow clusters of seeds indoors in February or March at 65°F or above. The tiny seedlings grow slowly. Set them out when the garden soil has warmed, allowing 6 inches between plants. Mulch with grass clippings or other material to control weeds.

PESTS AND DISEASES: Marjoram has never had a problem in my garden.

HARVEST AND PRESERVATION: Harvest sweet marjoram when buds are beginning to form. Place sprigs in a dehydrator, or hang in small bunches to dry. Then strip the leaves and store in airtight containers.

IN THE KITCHEN: The saying "When in doubt, use marjoram" expresses this herb's versatility. Casseroles, omelettes, cheese spreads, salad dressings, chicken, fish, lamb dishes, soups, tomatoes, and beans all benefit from a little of this herb. Try it in spaghetti sauce and Italian seasoning blends, and as the signature flavor of osso bucco. Or create a delicious Lebanese specialty of marjoram, parsley, green onion, basil, tomato, and bulgur wheat, blended like pesto and eaten with pita bread.

ORNAMENTAL USES: There is nothing quite like the little knotted flowers of marjoram. Although oregano looks somewhat similar, marjoram does not spread, allowing you to plant it freely either low in a border or in the kitchen garden. Its compact shape makes it an excellent choice for container gardens and window boxes. Use marjoram to scent gardens.

Mint

Mint. Labiatae (Mint family). *Mentha citrata* (orange mint); M. × *piperata* (peppermint), M. × *piperata* 'Blue Balsam'; M. *spicata* (spearmint) 'Crispa' (curly); M. *suaveolens* (apple mint), M. *suaveolens* 'Variegata' (pineapple mint); M. *requienii* (Corsican mint), and others.

DESCRIPTION: Mints are usually recognized by their menthol aroma, square stems, smooth pointed leaves, lavender or white flowers, and habit of spreading rapidly by underground leafless stems (stolons). Plants are perennial, most growing from 1 to 4 feet high, and they can easily take over even a large area. The tremendous variation among species and varieties of mints is reflected in the USDA collection, which numbers nearly 600.

Spearmint has bright green, pointed leaves, white flowers, and a clean, light scent. Curly or crispy mint is a spearmint variety with attractive pebbled, twisted leaves. Peppermint has dark green, pointed leaves with reddish veins and stems, lavender flowers, and a deeper mint scent. Dark, rounded leaves, purple flowers, and a refreshing citrus aroma characterize orange mint. Pineapple mint has smaller variegated green and white leaves, white flowers, and a mild fruity scent. All these varieties grow from 18 to 30 inches tall.

In contrast, apple mint has large, hairy, rounded leaves, white flowers, and a sweet menthol aroma, and can reach 5 feet tall; the tiny soft leaves of Corsican mint, emitting 'a powerful crème-de-menthe fragrance, creep along the ground, barely reaching 2 inches tall.

Although all mints are perennial, Corsican mint sometimes dies out in winter.

PROPAGATION AND CARE: Widely adaptable, mint will grow in any moderately fertile soil in full sun to full shade. Ample water is its most important requirement, and it tolerates damp areas well.

Many mints have sterile seeds or require cross-pollination with other varieties, and do not produce offspring that duplicate the parent. Propagate plants by dividing the roots and planting pieces of stolon; alternatively, root stem cuttings in water or sterile potting mix.

Because mint can take over a garden quickly, plant it in pots or contained areas. Cut back the roots with a sharp spade during spring and fall to keep the plants under control. In winter, when the plants die back to the ground, clip or mow the spent stalks to keep the garden tidy. Early spring is an excellent time to trim back the beds and move plants.

PESTS AND DISEASES: Although insects seldom bother mint, on rare occasions garden webworms shred the leaves. Thuricide is an effective control against feeding worms.

Mints are susceptible to soilborne viruses and rust. Light-colored patches on the leaves and stunted growth indicate virus, and orange to brown dots on the lower stems and undersides of leaves signal rust. Do not move affected plants to other areas or the disease will spread. For control, avoid fertilizing with fresh manure and clean up garden debris in the fall. You can harvest and use plant tips that are not diseased.

HARVEST AND PRESERVATION: Pinch back mint tips for garnishes as required to keep the stems bushy and delay flowering. Cut back plants to the ground when flowers begin forming, and they will produce a second and third crop. Hang the mint in bunches to dry—it will scent your entire house.

IN THE KITCHEN: Few flavors are more refreshing than the clean, cool taste of mint. Spearmint and apple mint are most popular for kitchen use in tabouli, split pea soup, fruit salads, new potatoes, mint juleps, punches, and other dishes. Any mint can be used for hot or iced tea. Peppermint has a reputation for curing tummy aches, but spearmint, orange mint, and apple mint are equally delicious. Dried mint leaves and oil are also used in potpourris, toothpaste, shampoo, face masques, and other cosmetics.

ORNAMENTAL USES: Because of their growth habit, mints are suitable for the wet, shady problem areas found in many maritime Northwest gardens. Varieties such as pineapple mint, curly mint, and 'Blue Balsam' peppermint are very ornamental in containers, especially when blooming. Corsican mint, with its fine tiny leaves and spreading habit, makes an excellent ground cover; plant it between paving stones and enjoy the intense aroma released when leaves are crushed while you walk along garden paths.

Nasturtium

Indian cress. Tropaeolaceae (Nasturtium family). *Tropaeolum majus*: trailing forms 'Empress of India', 'Glorious Gleam', 'Tall Trailing Mix'; compact forms 'Alaska', 'Whirlybird'.

DESCRIPTION: Cheery, adaptable nasturtiums deserve a place in container and garden herb plantings alike. These quick-growing annuals have flat, rounded leaves like diminutive lily pads, which grow along brittle stems from a fleshy root.

Nasturtium flowers are frilly, with or without spurs, and brightly colored in yellow, orange, cream, pink, mahogany, and other shades. Trailing varieties such as 'Tall Trailing' and 'Glorious Gleam' have brilliant blooms in many colors with pointed spurs. They can be trained to climb or trail, or simply allowed to spread. 'Empress of India' has bright scarlet flowers and dark green leaves. 'Whirlybird' is compact; its spurless, multicolored flowers face upward. 'Alaska' has bicolor green-and-white leaves, compact growth, and yellow or orange flowers. All varieties of nasturtium reseed themselves lavishly. Twin oval seeds are encased in a sheath at the end of flower stems.

PROPAGATION AND CARE: Nasturtiums like fairly rich, well-drained soil with steady moisture and tolerate full sun to full shade, although they grow best in partial shade. They flower freely through the summer months but are killed by the first hard frost.

Before sowing, soak the seed overnight, then plant it indoors in March, or wait until early May and plant directly outside. Seedling leaves are round and flat, about the size of a quarter.

PESTS AND DISEASES: Aphids like nasturtiums and often congregate on flower spurs and the undersides of leaves. Regular spraying with insecticidal soap will eliminate the problem.

HARVEST AND PRESERVATION: Use fresh nasturtium leaves and flowers, since they lose their flavor and texture when dried. Check closely for aphids, especially late in the season, and wash before using.

IN THE KITCHEN: The whole nasturtium plant has an agreeable peppery flavor suggestive of watercress. Use the blossoms as a bright garnish for salads and entrees or stuff them with cream cheese. Chop the flowers with the leaves to make colorful and tasty herb butter or cream cheese spreads. The leaves, especially variegated ones, also add interest to mixed green salads and can replace lettuce in sandwiches. Pickled flower buds and unripe seedpods are delicious caper substitutes—add a handful to jars of dilled cucumbers or green beans. Flowers, leaves, and stems steeped in white wine vinegar make a delicate flavoring delicious with chicken, salmon, and salads.

ORNAMENTAL USES: Nasturtiums have much to offer as ornamentals and would be worth growing even without their other uses. They delineate or fill in areas quickly and have a long blooming season, in addition to the bonus of shade tolerance. At Silver Bay Herb Farm, I fill in shady spots with nasturtiums after spring bulbs have finished, sowing in May and again in July for continuous bloom.

Compact varieties are great for edging and lend the garden an air of gaiety when their full color range is used. Massed nasturtiums provide an eye-stopping display of color. Combine them with blue bachelor's buttons for added pizzazz, or narrow your palette and highlight one of the unusual new colors such as cherry rose, salmon, or cream.

Grow trailing varieties to cover the ground, scramble up a trellis, or spill over the edge of planters or hanging baskets. The public plantings at the British Columbia–Washington State border at Blaine, Washington, include a great profusion of nasturtiums cascading down a steep slope.

Oregano

Oregano. Labiatae (Mint family). *O. heracleoticum* (Greek oregano); *O. vulgare* (common, wild): 'Aureum' (golden), 'Silver Anniversary'.

DESCRIPTION: The many varieties of oregano are part of a large, somewhat perplexing genus that also includes marjoram; over the years many attempts have been made to clarify its considerable confusion. What is generally recognized as the oregano of the kitchen is a 12- to 18-inch perennial with shallow creeping roots and small, dark green, opposite leaves on many stems. White or purple flowers clustered at the stem tips produce abundant seed, which scatters in the garden, resulting in new plants that may not duplicate the parent plant.

I always advise my customers to taste a leaf before choosing an oregano plant because flavors vary considerably. Greek oregano, which has white flowers, is the strongest variety. Italian oregano has a sweeter flavor reminiscent of sweet marjoram; it is not reliably winter hardy. Pot marjoram (wild oregano) is readily grown from seed, but has a bland flavor. Golden oregano and creeping golden marjoram have chartreuse leaves. 'Silver Anniversary' oregano is a pretty and hardy low-growing variety with green-and-white variegation.

PROPAGATION AND CARE: A tough plant, oregano tolerates poor soil, drought, harsh sun, high temperatures, and freezing cold. Give it a fertile, well-drained soil and a sunny location, and it will multiply prodigiously. Oregano's ability to thrive in arid conditions makes it a natural choice for hot, dry areas. Although culinary oreganos have their place in kitchen gardens, beware their spreading habit.

In his quest for the best-flavored oregano, Richard McCain of Quail Mountain Herbs in California planted a 100-foot row of Greek oregano seeds. Up came short and tall oreganos, oreganos with different sizes and colors of leaves, and even a few stray mint plants. As he demonstrated, it *is* possible to grow oregano from seed, but good results are more predictable with cuttings or root divisions. Use a sharp spade or knife to divide 3-year-old plants in spring or fall, and you will soon have vigorous new ones.

Keep grasses, dandelions, and other weeds out of your oregano plants, especially when they are just emerging from dormancy. Cut them back severely once or twice each season for a neat appearance. After the plants die down for winter, remove the dead stems with clippers or a string trimmer.

PESTS AND DISEASES: Oregano is not usually susceptible to insect damage, and diseases are seldom a problem. You may, however, find slugs hiding in cool places at the base of plants.

HARVEST AND PRESERVATION: Pick oregano for the table anytime during the growing season. Use the tender tips or strip the leaves from woody stems. As flower buds begin to form, cut plants back to the ground, fasten bunches with rubber bands, and hang them to air dry. If your oregano blooms, do not despair—the leaves are still very pungent. Oregano is easy to dry and keeps its flavor well.

IN THE KITCHEN: Spaghetti sauce, pizza, salsa, and pasta salads just do not taste right without oregano. It also enhances chicken, meat loaf, soups, Greek salads, corn on the cob, roasted red bell peppers, and other vegetable dishes.

ORNAMENTAL USES: Pretty but hard-to-find golden oregano and the recently introduced 'Silver Anniversary' are both choice low-growing ornamentals. Creeping golden marjoram (considered to be an oregano) is more readily available, and its bright color contrasts dramatically with darker leaves. You can hang varied bunches of dried oregano in the kitchen for decoration. Florists use the flowers fresh or dried in arrangements.

Parsley

Parsley. Umbelliferae (Carrot family). *Petroselinum crispum* var. *crispum* (curled parsley): 'Moss Curled', 'Triple Curled', 'Afro', 'Darki'; *P. crispum* var. *neapolitanum* (Italian parsley): 'Giant Italian' or 'Gigante d'Italia'.

DESCRIPTION: Curled and Italian parsley, both biennials, are very popular with gardeners. Parsley is such a favorite that many seed catalogs include it with the vegetables or devote a special section to it. The plant forms a rosette of deep green leaves about 12 inches tall during its first year. The leaves emerge tightly curled from the center, unfurling gradually while newer leaves appear. The white, fleshy root tapers like a carrot. The second year, a branched seed stalk rises to about 3 feet, topped with umbels of small yellow flowers. When pointed brown seeds ripen, the plant's life cycle is complete. Italian parsley is similar in all respects except that its leaves are flat and deeply lobed, not curled. Some cooks prefer its fine flavor.

PROPAGATION AND CARE: Grow parsley in rich soil with ample water and full sun or partial shade. Before planting, soak parsley seed overnight, then sow indoors in February or March for early plants. Seeds germinate slowly; folk wisdom holds that parsley goes to the devil and back seven times before it can sprout. The first leaves are narrow and pointed; subsequent leaves are characteristically curly or lobed. Transplant young seedlings carefully in early spring for best results.

Seeds can be sown directly in the garden in March or April, although fast-growing weeds can easily overtake young plants. Parsley reseeds abundantly; some gardeners who never bother planting it always have plenty.

Left outdoors, parsley overwinters easily in the maritime Northwest. Plants go dormant and begin growing again in early spring.

For year-round harvest, pot up a few plants in October or November and bring them indoors. You can prolong the life of your parsley by breaking off the seed stalk when it appears, but eventually the plant will go to seed, and the leaves will develop a strong, bitter flavor.

PESTS AND DISEASES: Parsley is seldom affected by insect pests or diseases. Root rust can be a problem, but has never affected my plants.

HARVEST AND PRESERVATION: When picking parsley, grasp one of the lower stalks and pull it gently downward while giving a little twist. The stalk comes away where it meets the plant, leaving no piece behind to rot. Use this method consistently; picking will be easier and cleaner.

To keep parsley fresh, place whole stems in a small amount of water in a glass jar and refrigerate. To preserve parsley for future use, chop it and dry it in the microwave, dehydrator, or oven (on the lowest setting with the door open a crack). Store dried parsley away from light to preserve the bright green color.

IN THE KITCHEN: Rich in vitamin C, vitamin A, and iron, parsley has a fresh, versatile flavor. It is excellent in soups, quiches, tabouli, falafel, salads, and any savory dish. When it is added during the last minutes of cooking, color and nutrients are retained at their peak. Try placing a small bowl of chopped parsley on the table so diners can help themselves.

ORNAMENTAL USES: Since the days of the ancient Greeks, parsley has been used as a border plant. It can make a lush yet tidy edging of refreshing deep green around the entire garden or along a path. In a kitchen garden or planter, it remains compact for the first year. The second year, however, it grows very tall; remove it unless you like the airy, branching appearance. Beneficial insects love the flowers, as with other umbelliferous plants.

Rose Geranium

Sweet-scented geranium. Geraniaceae (Geranium family). *Pelargonium graveolens*: 'Attar of Roses', 'Cinnamon Rose', 'Lady Plymouth', 'Lilac Rose', 'Old-Fashioned Rose', 'Rober's Lemon Rose', and others; *P. radens*: 'Dr. Livingston', 'Skeleton Rose', and others.

DESCRIPTION: Start your exploration of the many scented geraniums with rose geraniums. These tender perennials, native to South Africa, belong to a classification of pelargoniums prized for their scent rather than their blossoms. Their deeply lobed, veined leaves contain high concentrations of essential oils with a powerful rose aroma. Small pink flowers appear in bunches at the tops of the jointed stems, which become woody with age. Mature plants grow upward of 3 feet tall and with winter protection can live for many years.

The 'Old-Fashioned Rose' variety is probably the most popular of all scented geraniums. People are often astonished when they first smell the strong rose odor of its leaves. Years of breeding have resulted in more than 50 other rose varieties, each having a different leaf shape and scent. 'Skeleton Rose' and the variegated 'Lady Plymouth' are quite distinctive, and 'Attar of Rose' is noted for its marvelous fragrance. The scent of roses is mingled with other aromas in 'Lemon Rose', 'Cinnamon Rose', and 'Lilac Rose'. These and other scented geraniums, which smell like anything from peppermint and lemon to musk and apple cider, are an altogether fascinating group of plants.

PROPAGATION AND CARE: Give rose geraniums good, well-drained soil and full sun. These drought-tolerant plants like to dry out completely between waterings. Like other geraniums, they rarely survive winters outside. In October, when nights become cold, bring them into a frost-free area such as the house, garage, or a cool greenhouse.

To propagate, take stem cuttings from soft growth in early spring and fall. Cut directly across a node and place the cutting in a mixture of sand and perlite. A source of bottom heat is helpful, if available. After plants root, in four to six weeks, transfer them to a richer potting mix or directly to the ground.

Rose geraniums make excellent container plants. Although they get big, they do not mind being root bound. They can be left in pots and sunk into the ground, but will grow much larger if planted directly into the garden. Some people grow them as houseplants in a sunny window year-round.

Pinch flowers back to encourage bushy growth on your rose geraniums. When you dig plants in the fall, cut them back by a third (dry or root the trimmings). Store them where they will not freeze in dampened peat, singly in pots or together in a large tub. Water only enough to keep them alive through the winter, about once a month. When new growth begins to form, usually in February, prune the plants back by at least half to keep them compact. Water more frequently as the plants come out of dormancy. Gradually harden them off and set them outside in mid-May to June when the weather is warm and settled.

PESTS AND DISEASES: Aphids can be a real problem on rose geraniums, especially when they are in an enclosed area. Spray insecticidal soap as needed to keep pests in check.

HARVEST AND PRESERVATION: Shape your rose geranium plants as you harvest the leaves, cutting or pinching them back to a leaf node. Use leaves fresh, hang in bunches, or dry in a dehydrator and store for later use.

IN THE KITCHEN: Rose geraniums have a flavor to match their lovely scent, making them valuable in the kitchen, especially for desserts. When baking a white, pound, or angel food cake, line the bottom of a greased pan with leaves before pouring in the batter (remove before serving). Or bury the leaves in sugar to scent it for use in muffins and scones. Rose geranium jelly is another favorite; add a leaf to each pint jar when making apple jelly. Try steeping the leaves in warm sugar syrup as a flavoring for sliced strawberries, lemonade, and frosting on sugar cookies.

ORNAMENTAL USES: Rose geraniums in the garden contribute luxurious fragrance and beauty. Position them where they are accessible, lining a path or beside a well-used garden bench. Or grow them on a deck or patio, where you can reach out and crush a leaf. Large planters of rose geraniums make an entryway memorable, and they are always lovely grouped with roses and other fragrant flowers. These quick growers are also great for filling in empty spots. Sometimes I set out pots containing large scented geraniums to hide gaps where sage or other herbs have been cut back.

Rosemary

Rosemary. Labiatae (Mint family). *Rosmarinus officinalis*: 'Albus', 'Arp', 'Huntington Carpet', 'Majorca', 'Miss Jessup's Upright', 'Prostratus', 'Santa Barbara', 'Tuscan Blue', and others.

DESCRIPTION: Rosemary is a long-lived evergreen perennial, which can reach about 6 feet tall, although prostrate varieties creep along the ground at only 6 inches in height. Several large branches grow from a single stem attached to a spreading root system.

The dark green, glossy leaves of rosemary are opposite, narrow, and pointed, with a pine aroma. Flowers, which are borne up the stems, are usually blue, less commonly pink or white, and like other blossoms in the mint family, look like little orchids. In the maritime Northwest, rosemary blooms in April and May.

R. officinalis or common rosemary has an excellent flavor for cooking. 'Arp', a relatively new selection, is hardy to about 15°F. 'Tuscan Blue' has narrow leaves, thick columnar growth, a sweet rosemary fragrance, and bright blue flowers. 'Alba' has white flowers, and 'Majorca' has pink ones. 'Miss Jessup's Upright' is a good hedge plant. Of the prostrate or trailing varieties, the vigorous 'Santa Barbara' is most widely available; 'Huntington Carpet' is a small-leaved variety with blue flowers. Both need winter protection.

Rosemary is often used in shampoos and hair rinses, especially for brunettes. It gives an herbal scent to potpourris and is popular in bath mixtures as a fragrant muscle relaxant.

PROPAGATION AND CARE: Native to the Mediterranean, rosemary thrives in dry, well-drained soil. Give your plants full sun for as much of the day as possible. For best results in acid Northwest soils, work in about ¼ cup of agricultural lime when planting and again each spring. Ordinarily, plants do not need watering in the garden, but container-grown rosemary does. Plants will not survive if their roots dry out completely or stand in water, so you must strike a balance.

Rosemary can be grown from seed, although germination can be erratic and seedlings grow very slowly, even with bottom heat. The first leaves are oval; true leaves are narrow with typical rosemary veining. Most gardeners get better results by taking cuttings in midsummer or by purchasing plants. Another method is to layer an established rosemary by scraping a little bark from the underside of a branch, then pegging it to the ground. When roots form, cut the new plant from the parent and replant it.

Rosemary is almost a maintenance-free herb. Whatever pruning or shaping you may wish to do can be accomplished by judicious harvesting. Mature rosemary can compete with most weeds, but do keep grass and other pernicious weeds away from your plants.

Until it has a well-established root system (three to four years), rosemary will not reliably survive winters in the maritime Northwest. Most varieties should be potted up and wintered in a garage or cool greenhouse when they are small. Larger plants usually survive but may lose some branches. To protect them, mulch the roots with dry leaves, straw, or other materials and, if you want to be especially solicitous, throw an old blanket over the plants when nighttime temperatures fall to 20°F. Rake off the mulch in early to mid-March. Trailing rosemary is even less hardy than upright and hardly ever survives a Northwest winter.

PESTS AND DISEASES: Rosemary seldom has insect or disease problems. Leafhoppers can yellow plants outdoors and spider mites sometimes attack plants grown inside; use insecticidal soap sprays for control.

HARVEST AND PRESERVATION: Pick tender, pale stems of new growth for the finest rosemary. Stems remain short until after plants bloom, but can grow almost a foot tall over the season. Although rosemary is evergreen, it goes dormant in the winter; harvest plants only lightly during this season, especially when young, so that harvesting does not outstrip their ability to regenerate and grow larger. If you cut woody stems, strip off the leaves and use for cooking; discard stems. Rosemary dries well when hung in small bunches in a very warm, airy place.

IN THE KITCHEN: The warm, resinous flavor of rosemary enhances pork, lamb, and beef. Try grilling lamb, fruit kabobs, or new potatoes on rosemary skewers for an impressive presentation. Rosemary is the signature flavor of minestrone soup and indispensable in many other Italian specialties. Split pea soup, fried potatoes, carrots, fresh orange slices, herb vinegars, biscuits, and shortbread are also delicious with rosemary.

ORNAMENTAL USES: Because it is evergreen and has good vertical lines, rosemary is effective in garden design. A pair of rosemary plants placed beside a gate or other entrance extends a special welcome to garden visitors. A tall plant makes a handsome focal point in the center of a formal herb garden and grows more quickly than a bay tree. Rosemary also can add interesting height and texture to gardens in whiskey barrels or large clay pots. Prostrate varieties are lovely cascading from planter boxes or hanging baskets and also soften the edges of concrete steps and rock walls.

Although a gardener must be patient, a hedge of mature rosemary is worth a few years' wait. Clipped, such a hedge provides a beautiful edging; allowed to grow tall, it is a splendid garden divider or screen, and all the more appealing if a nearby bench allows enjoyment of the rosemary fragrance and honeybees busy amid the tiny flowers. 'Miss Jessup's Upright' is a strong-growing, free-flowering variety that forms a neat bush suitable for hedges.

Both upright and prostrate rosemary are good choices for topiaries. It's fun to train them to resemble small, bushy trees or to use wire or wooden forms to create cones, hearts, or other fanciful shapes. Rosemary has long been associated with Christmas, and potted plants make pretty little evergreen Christmas trees.

Sage

Sage. Labiatae (Mint family). *Salvia elegans* (pineapple); *S. officinalis* (common sage): 'Golden' or 'Aurea', 'Holt's Mammoth', 'Purpurascens' (purple), 'Tricolor'; *S. sclarea* (clary), and others.

DESCRIPTION: There are many members of the Salvia clan, including the ubiquitous bedding types. All have ornamental value, but those considered to be herbal are also valued in cooking or medicines. Sage comes with leaves of gray-blue, purple, gold and green variegation, and green, white, and pink-purple variegation.

Common sage is a hardy and often long-lived perennial, which grows to about 3 feet high. Its grayish green, pebbled leaves remain on the plant year-round. Left to grow untended, the stems become long and woody with leaves mainly at their tips. Purple flowers bloom like tiny snapdragons along a single spike. 'Holt's Mammoth' has a good flavor and larger leaves than common sage, which make it popular among commercial growers. Purple sage is distinguished by its purplish leaves. Golden sage has pretty, light green and gold variegation, is mildly flavored, and grows to 2 feet. 'Tricolor' is much like it in flavor and growth habit, but its colorful leaves are streaked with white, pink, and purple. Pineapple sage is quite different, with thin, smooth green leaves and a sweet pineapple scent; showy red flowers attract hummingbirds to the garden. Clary sage is dramatic, with hairy, pebbled leaves and a thick flower stalk, which can reach 5 feet. The blossoms have a curious musky odor valued in perfumery. Usually biennial, with excellent drainage it can live for several years.

PROPAGATION AND CARE: Most sage is hardy and needs no winter protection in the maritime Northwest. It thrives in almost any well-drained soil with abundant calcium, preferring a sunny spot, although it does well in dappled shade. Take care not to overwater container-grown sage; consider grouping it with other drought-tolerant herbs such as lavender and thyme.

Common sage is easily grown from seed sown in autumn or spring, from cuttings, or by pegging down the branches until they root.

To renew plants that are getting leggy, cut them back to about 5 inches high in early spring (usually March) when they begin to break dormancy. Fertilize them generously with an all-purpose fertilizer mix scratched in around the roots. New growth will soon begin from the base of the plants, and before long they will be beautifully bushy and compact. I first tried this technique on some straggly old plants I thought I would have to replace anyway, and liked the results so much I have done it ever since.

Pineapple sage roots readily from cuttings; it rarely survives maritime Northwest winters unless taken indoors.

PESTS AND DISEASES: Insects usually stay away from sage. Mildew, the most common disease problem, looks like a white powder on the leaves, and strikes when humidity is high and air circulation is poor. To avoid it, try spacing plants farther apart or spraying them with a solution of ¼ teaspoon of baking soda per quart of water.

HARVEST AND PRESERVATION: Harvest your sage twice each season. Cut the new growth, bunch it at the stems, and fasten with rubber bands. Hang the bunches to dry in an airy room. Alternatively, use a food dehydrator for drying.

IN THE KITCHEN: Fresh sage has a far more delicate flavor than dried, and it is a shame to relegate it to stuffing mixes for poultry. Used with a light hand, sage can be delightful in breads, cheese spreads, poultry, or pork dishes. Italian cooks use sage with liver and veal; in England it is favored for cheeses, sausages, and "savoury dishes." For a new twist on the sage-and-turkey theme, grind the herb fresh with turkey for low-fat grilled "burgers." Fresh or dried, sage also makes a delicious and healthful tea. Bunches of dried sage, with their gray-green color and twisted leaf shapes, make homey kitchen decorations. They are also good for herbal wreaths and everlasting bouquets.

ORNAMENTAL USES: All sage has ornamental value, making it an ideal landscaping herb. Its rounded shape makes it a good contrast to vertical growers such as fennel; its medium height makes it suitable in many places. Sage plants of various colors grouped together make an interesting garden vignette. Because leaves remain on the plant year-round, sage can help define the structure of a garden in winter as well as summer. Clary sage massed is a showstopper in the garden when the large, bending flower stalks gradually become erect and covered with soft purple blossoms.

Savory

Savory. Labiatae (Mint family). *Satureja hortensis* (summer savory); *S. montana* (winter savory).

DESCRIPTION: Summer and winter savory are closely related plants with a pungent, versatile flavor. Their leaves are glossy, dark green, and narrow, and dainty pinkish flowers bloom in whorls along the upper parts of the stems. Their root systems are fibrous but not spreading.

Summer savory is an annual that grows to about 18 inches. Its leaves are about 1 inch long and spaced 1 inch apart along the stems, giving the plant a somewhat open, bushy look. Stems are tinged with red. It is more aromatic in the garden and has a more delicate flavor than winter savory.

Winter savory is a hardy, evergreen, long-lived perennial. Its appearance is dense and compact, with more-closely spaced leaves and lower growth than summer savory. Stems become woody with age, and their diameter increases gradually as the plant grows outward and layers. A mature winter savory can be more than 2 feet across and 1 foot tall when in bloom.

PROPAGATION AND CARE: An adaptable herb, savory flourishes in a well-drained, poor to moderately rich soil. It likes full sun and is a good candidate for a hot spot in the garden. Winter savory needs no protection from cold weather in the maritime Northwest.

Summer and winter savory are easy to grow and can be started from seed sown indoors in March, or in the ground from mid-April to May. Both self-seed readily. Germination takes one to three weeks and is quickest in warm temperatures. Seedlings have a weedy appearance with small pointed leaves, so take care not to pull them up by mistake. Winter savory can also be propagated by cuttings or layering.

Allow about 12 inches between summer savory plants, and stake them if necessary to keep them upright. Space the slower-growing winter savory 6 inches apart, and thin as it fills in an area. Prune plants in early spring to prevent sprawling, and trim off spent flower stalks to keep a neat appearance.

PESTS AND DISEASES: Hardly anything bothers savory!

HARVEST AND PRESERVATION: Cut or pinch back sprigs of savory to use as needed—the evergreen winter species is particularly welcome during the cold months. When buds are forming on summer savory, cut the plants back to about 3 inches from the ground. They will regrow for a second harvest.

Savory dries well on screens or hung in bunches. When harvesting for everlasting bouquets, wait until the plants are in full bloom. You can pull up entire summer savory plants at the end of the season and hang them to dry.

IN THE KITCHEN: Savory is aptly named; its lively, versatile flavor goes with practically any savory dish. This good blending herb is used in Italian, Provençal, poultry, and other seasoning mixtures. Try it with meats, soups, casseroles, and vegetables. The oils in savory aid digestion, perhaps explaining why it is commonly paired with legumes in German cooking; summer savory goes with fresh peas and beans, winter savory with dried.

ORNAMENTAL USES: Although summer savory has a somewhat rangy habit, its flavor earns this herb a place in the kitchen or vegetable garden. Planted closely and kept clipped, winter savory also can be a handsome edging plant or a structural element in a formal knot garden. As a low-growing evergreen, it deserves to be in nearly any year-round herb garden.

Sweet Cicely

British myrrh. Umbelliferae (Carrot family). *Myrrhis odorata.*

DESCRIPTION: Sweet cicely is a graceful perennial. Its downy leaves, made up of several pairs of finely cut leaflets, are reminiscent of the familiar bracken fern. Mature plants are 2 to 3 feet tall with large, fleshy taproots reaching deep into the soil.

Umbels of delicately fragrant white flowers bloom from May to June. The large, dark brown, ribbed seeds are 1 inch long. All parts of the plant have a pleasant licorice flavor. Plants are long-lived and among the hardiest of herbs.

PROPAGATION AND CARE: Sweet cicely is an excellent plant for maritime Northwest gardens. It prefers a crumbly, moist soil with good drainage, the sort found around old fruit trees. Enrich a poor soil with compost or manure. This decorative plant requires little maintenance and grows beautifully in shade. Without shade at least part of the day, the leaves tend to wither. At Silver Bay, a patch has grown and spread on the shady side of an outbuilding for more than 40 years.

Begin with a plant, or sow the freshest seed available. Seedlings are about 3 inches high, with a lacy, triangular true leaf between two narrow first leaves. The roots can be dug and divided in fall or early spring—make sure each division has an eye at the top.

After plants bloom, the leaves turn yellow and shrivel up. Cut plants back severely and they will put forth new leaves. Leaves die back in autumn; clean them up and cut off seed heads or leave them to disappear and reseed on their own by spring.

PESTS AND DISEASES: Pests have never damaged the sweet cicely that I have grown.

HARVEST AND PRESERVATION: The flavor of sweet cicely is too delicate to survive drying or freezing; the fresh herb is best. Pinch off tender leaflets by hand from February through October, or cut the stems with scissors if a larger supply is needed.

Harvest seeds for planting when they are dark and heavy. Sow them immediately, or dry them on screens for a few days and store in the freezer (to prolong viability).

IN THE KITCHEN: This aptly named herb contains natural sweeteners that help to neutralize acids in tart fruits. If you add 1 tablespoon of chopped stems and leaves per cup of fruit in rhubarb cakes and compotes, applesauce, and similar dishes, you can cut the sugar by half.

Sweet cicely makes an acceptable substitute for chervil, which has a similar light licorice flavor but is a short-lived annual. Use chopped or small leaves in green or fruit salads, or to garnish soups. Add 3 tablespoons to your favorite biscuit or shortbread recipe for an intriguing flavor. Pick the young seeds to nibble as an herbal breath freshener or add them to fruit salad.

ORNAMENTAL USES: Sweet cicely offers a good solution to a shady problem area in the garden. The lacy leaves and dainty white flowers, while not showy, are quietly ornamental, looking their best when not much is blooming in some gardens. They add textural interest to the back of a border and act as an effective foil for nasturtiums and other low-growing herbs. Once established, plants can go rampant. Dig them out while they're young to control spreading.

Tarragon

Tarragon. Compositae (Aster family). *Artemisia dracunculus* var. *sativa* (French tarragon); *A. dracunculoides* (Russian tarragon).

DESCRIPTION: French tarragon is a hardy perennial, which dies back to the ground in winter. Its Latin name and French nickname, meaning "the little dragon," are thought to derive from its serpentine roots. In March or April, tarragon sends up new shoots, which grow 12 to 15 inches. Its narrow, pointed leaves have a flavor reminiscent of licorice. The tiny green flowers are inconspicuous and do not produce viable seeds. Russian tarragon, a related herb, is so vigorous it can reach 4 feet. Although it does set seed, the flavor is so inferior that it is seldom grown.

PROPAGATION AND CARE: Tarragon, more particular than some other herbs, prefers a fairly rich soil with full sun and ample moisture. Good drainage is essential. Tarragon is very hardy, and the plants actually need a period of cold and dormancy every year. In cold, wet soil, however, the roots rot and the plants cannot survive. Occasionally, gardeners find that their tarragon plants will not flourish. Try two or three different areas to see where the plants do best.

Plant division is the most practical way to propagate tarragon, since seed is unavailable and cuttings require special greenhouse equipment. Dig 3-year-old plants while they are dormant (October to

February) and tease the roots apart, taking care not to break the brittle shoots. Make sure you have at least two eyes or shoots on each piece. The new plants will mature in about three years.

Fertilize established plants in the spring by scratching in ½ cup of all-purpose fertilizer mix around each plant. Keep them well weeded, since quack grass, sourgrass, and other pernicious weeds can overtake a bed of tarragon quickly. Leave the dead stems to mark the location of the plants during the winter if you like, but do clip them off when new growth begins to make harvesting easier.

PESTS AND DISEASES: Slugs like the tender emerging shoots of tarragon and can destroy young plants. Bait and other methods are helpful, but again, keep the plants clear of weeds, which provide shady hiding places.

HARVEST AND PRESERVATION: Pinch tarragon sprigs from early spring on. When the plants have reached full growth and leaf tips begin to turn yellow, cut them back to about 2 inches from the ground. Fertilize the plants lightly with regular-strength fish fertilizer, and they will produce a second and perhaps a third crop.

Preserving the bright green color and strong flavor of tarragon can be a challenge. Air drying in bunches is often disappointing, but the additional heat provided by a dehydrator gives better results, as do freezing and microwaving. Steep 1 cup of tarragon sprigs in a quart of white wine vinegar to make a tasty condiment, or to pickle sprigs in the French manner, wash and pack them tightly into clean pint jars and fill with white wine vinegar. Use the leaves as for fresh; the concentrated vinegar is a fabulous flavoring too.

IN THE KITCHEN: A classic cooking herb, tarragon is delicious with chicken, fish, oysters, eggs, pâtés, and aspics. It is indispensable in béarnaise, hollandaise, and tartar sauces, and in salad dressings such as Green Goddess. Add chopped tarragon to asparagus spears, green beans, mushrooms, and carrots, and use it to flavor pickled asparagus spears and the tiny, sour cucumber pickles known as cornichons.

ORNAMENTAL USES: Tarragon's vibrant green color and upright habit make it a fine choice for planter boxes, and it has a place in any kitchen and herb garden. Harvest the plants regularly to keep them from becoming yellow and unattractive.

Thyme

Thyme. Labiatae (Mint family). *Thymus* × *citriodorus* (lemon): 'Argenteus Variegatus' (variegated lemon), 'Doone Valley'; *T. herba-barona* (caraway); *T. praecox* ssp. *arcticus* (creeping); *T. pseudolanugino-sus* (woolly); *T. serpyllum* (wild); *T. vulgaris* (common): 'Argenteus' (silver), 'Aureus' (gold), English, French, Porlock.

DESCRIPTION: There are well over 200 varieties of thyme, all peren-nial, and most are very hardy. Many are descended from plants that grow wild around the Mediterranean. The most productive one for culi-nary purposes is English or common thyme, a hardy evergreen shrub that grows to about 12 inches tall. Its small, opposite, dark green leaves are strongly aromatic. Bees are attracted to the whorls of pink flowers that bloom in April and May; stems become woody with age. Seeds are tiny, round, and brown to black.

French thyme has narrower, grayish leaves and less compact growth than English thyme. Many cooks prefer its flavor over that of other varieties. Porlock thyme is an improved English type with dark leaves and a dense habit. Silver thyme has beautiful variegated leaves and blossoms, similar growth habit, and a more delicate flavor than English thyme. Lemon thymes vary in coloration, leaf size, and growth habit, but all have a fresh, citrus flavor. They are generally less vigorous and hardy than *vulgaris* types. Golden thyme is a chartreuse creeping variety forming compact mounds about 6 inches high with inconspicuous white flowers; it looks good all year. Common creeping thyme has pink flowers and spreads via roots along the stems. Other varieties of creeping thyme have white, red, or lavender blossoms. Caraway thyme has small, deep green leaves and the pronounced flavor of its namesake. Woolly thyme is the lowest growing of all, a silvery, ground-hugging mat with minute, downy leaves.

PROPAGATION AND CARE: One of the least demanding of herbs, thyme thrives in average to poor soil with partial or full sun. This tough plant can cope with heat, drought, and cold. Good drainage is essential.

English and French thymes are easily grown from seed sown in flats or seedbeds early in the spring. The seedlings look like tiny sprigs of thyme and need careful weeding if grown outside. Potting two or three together produces sizable plants more quickly. The plants grow to about 8 inches in diameter the first season. Replace them after three or four years when the stems have become woody.

Commercially, thyme is propagated by cuttings or root division, since seeds do not always duplicate the parent plant. Take cuttings from late spring through fall. When older plants become sparse in the cen-ters, divide them with a sharp shovel in fall or early spring.

To keep thyme plants shapely, prune them lightly in February before new growth begins. I have found no need for mulching or other protection in the mild winters of the maritime Northwest.

PESTS AND DISEASES: Slugs can do damage, so watch for them. Generally, however, all varieties of thyme are pest and disease free.

HARVEST AND PRESERVATION: Cut or pinch sprigs year-round for kitchen use. As plants begin budding, clip them back to 2 inches from the ground. New growth appears quickly. Hang the thyme in bundles or spread it on screens to dry. When brittle, hold the bundles over a sheet of news-paper and rub the leaves from the stems, then store in glass jars. If you plan to use your thyme for wreaths or other ornamental purposes, harvest it in bloom—the flowers dry to a rich lavender color.

IN THE KITCHEN: One of the most versatile of all herbs, thyme complements meats, poultry, fish, game, soups, and chowders. This wonderful blending herb is included in bouquets garnis, poultry seasoning, Italian blends, and French country herbs. It is delicious in mushroom and French onion soups, superb with sautéed chanterelles. Lemon thyme sparks up chicken, fish, and fruit desserts such as applesauce, rhubarb compote, and berry cobblers. The strong flavor of caraway thyme is good with roast beef, in breads, or in cream cheese spreads. Although edible, creeping thymes are seldom used for flavoring.

ORNAMENTAL USES: The many forms of thyme make it as versatile in the garden as in the kitchen. Leaves vary in texture and color from grays to greens and gold. Attractive flowers may be pink or white. The gently rounded English and French varieties are beautiful as edgings or interwoven among perennials in a border. They can also be clipped as elements in knot gardens and other formal designs. The soft look of silver thyme is particularly lovely when contrasted with bright flowers such as roses or plants with large, dark leaves. Creeping thymes, which have white, pink, red, or lavender flowers, star in rockeries, cascading down stairs or growing like a fragrant carpet among stepping-stones. Occasionally used in place of grass lawns, creeping thyme requires weeding, an activity that provides lessons in patience.

Monthly Northwest Herb Care

CHAPTER 6

Part of the pleasure of gardening is working in harmony with the seasons. The gardener learns to submit to nature's timetable, as each season inexorably flows into the next, bringing its own tasks and rewards.

Still, the dozens of chores that await the gardener, whatever the season or the weather, can be daunting. Before the busy growing season begins, start a garden journal for keeping daily or weekly records, taking notes, and mapping your planting diagrams—this has been invaluable to me as both a record and a reference. Use your time productively—if it is too soggy to work outdoors, clean seeds or tidy the shed. By keeping up steadily, you'll be rewarded with better results.

SPRING

Spring is one of the busiest seasons in the garden, when the earth awakens and new life stirs. "Spring work," as it is called on my farm, means sowing, watering, and tending seeds in the greenhouse, then hardening off and transplanting seedlings to the garden. It also means getting the garden beds in shape—digging, tilling, fertilizing, mulching paths—and sowing seeds or transplanting herbs. This work continues throughout the entire season.

MARCH This can be a fine, wild month, due to the vernal equinox. As the days warm up, gardening possibilities increase.

Garden checklist: Construct beds and paths if the weather allows. Till or dig over existing beds as soon as possible to dry out soggy soil and give green manures time to break down. Work compost and all-purpose fertilizer mix into the beds. Remove mulches covering your plants to allow air and sunlight to reach them.

Plant checklist: March is an excellent time to divide or move perennials and rearrange your garden. Divide perennials such as oregano, thyme, mint, and chives before they begin fast growth. Dig up and divide tarragon early, before the brittle pinkish shoots grow long.

Many kinds of seed can be safely planted indoors and out. Seed packets often instruct you to sow a certain number of weeks from the date of the last expected frost. In all but the coldest areas of the maritime Northwest, calculate back from April 30. Plant seeds of arugula, calendula, cilantro, dill, and fennel directly into the soil. Indoors, sow basil, lavender, marjoram, nasturtium, oregano, sage, and summer and winter savory. Keep track of sowing dates in your journal.

APRIL Gardening fever strikes! Spring is definitely here, but the weather is changeable. April showers usually make watering even seedling beds unnecessary. Remember that tender plants may be nipped by frost if set out too soon. Coax an earlier harvest out of many herbs either by covering individual plants with mini-greenhouses made of plastic milk jugs or protecting entire rows with spun-bonded polyester fabric. Wait to set out basil until the soil is warmer, unless you are a gambler willing to risk your first planting.

Garden checklist: Outdoors, keep working on garden beds and structure. Control slugs, which can do tremendous damage to seedlings.

Plant checklist: Sow arugula, cilantro, dill, nasturtium, and summer savory directly in the ground. Weed perennials regularly to avoid more tedious work later. Side-dress herbs with compost or all-purpose fertilizer by scratching it into the ground around the plants. Harvest perennial herbs that have overwintered. Enjoy the tender and delicious young leaves of chives, fennel, lemon balm, lovage, parsley, sweet cicely, and tarragon in spring salads. Prune rose geranium and add the leaves to teas, cakes, and syrups.

Late in the month, set out bay trees, pineapple sage, scented geraniums, and other plants that were wintered indoors. If the weather seems uncooperative, wait until mid-May to be on the safe side.

In the greenhouse, make a second sowing of basil early in the month. Keep a watchful eye on seedlings, watering regularly and transplanting them to larger pots if necessary to encourage steady growth. Harden off plants that are ready to go outside.

MAY If you are going to plant a small herb garden in a day or a weekend, the last weeks of this month are the time to do it. "The weather is settled," as the seed catalogs say, and "the soil has warmed." Frost is no longer a worry, and although one year an unseasonal hailstorm shredded most of my seedlings, by May it is usually safe to transplant all your seedlings or purchased plants outdoors.

Garden checklist: Transplant, sow, and weed. If possible, choose a calm, cloudy day to transplant basil and other seedlings. Bright sunlight can scald the leaves of plants that are not hardened off properly. Do not allow seedbeds to dry out, even if this means watering two or three times a day with a watering can.

Plant checklist: Fertilize plants with applications of regular solution fish emulsion or all-purpose fertilizer mix and keep watered to stimulate growth. Fennel, mint, oregano, sage, sweet cicely, tarragon, and other perennials will be sizable enough to harvest. "Volunteer" seedlings from last year's garden of calendula, chives, dill, fennel, nasturtium, oregano, parsley, summer savory, and thyme may have appeared by now, too. Leave them to grow in situ, transplant them to more appropriate places, or weed them out without mercy, as you choose.

Thyme and chives are among the earliest herbs to bloom. Cut back large thyme plants almost to the ground and hang the aromatic bunches to dry. Either cut back chives or harvest individual stems, discard plant debris, and hang to dry in bunches.

This year's seedlings of quick-growing arugula, cilantro, dill, savory, and other greens can be thinned and used in the kitchen. Make a second or third sowing of these herbs for continuous harvests.

SUMMER

Ah, salad days! This is the season to really enjoy your garden. Lavish your meals with an abundance of fresh herbs, and pick bouquets of fragrant herb blossoms for centerpieces and house decoration. If possible, set a couple of chairs or a picnic table near your herb patch, and take advantage of the fragrant atmosphere of your outdoor living room with family and guests.

JUNE The weather is often cool and cloudy this month, though warm spells are not uncommon. Once your direct-sown seedlings are up and transplants are getting established, maintenance is the key.

Garden checklist: Continue fertilizing perennials. Review your watering system; check hoses and sprinklers and consider investing in a timer or a drip system. Keep conditions favorable for young plants' optimum growth by watering and weeding steadily. Larger plants can successfully compete with weeds, but thoroughly go over the beds at least once to clean them up. Then mulch with grass clippings, straw, shredded newspaper, or other organic material to suppress weeds (if the weather is dry and slug populations are low).

Plant checklist: Begin picking basil. Make late sowings of arugula, basil, cilantro, and dill.

JULY Regularly take a walk around your garden, observing the growth, needs, and problems of your plants. As you become intimately familiar with your plants, garden priorities will become clear. Note in your journal observations about maturity dates, productivity, and any special characteristics of your plants. During this lush month, rewards are all around you.

Garden checklist: When the weather is hot, gardening tasks, particularly watering, are best done in the coolness of morning and evening.

Plant checklist: Harvest herbs before they flower, go to seed, and look unattractive. Most plants will put on new growth and yield a second harvest.

AUGUST As the herb garden reaches a crescendo, the supply seems endless. A hot spell when you can hear your basil growing is almost predictable.

Garden checklist: Early in the month, make one last sowing of cilantro and dill. Keep seedlings moist until germination takes place. Harvest, dry, and braid garlic. Sow green manure seeds such as crimson clover, vetch, or small-seeded fava beans for a cover crop in empty beds or underneath annuals such as basil and summer savory. Started while the weather is warm, green manure plants will blanket the ground with green in winter.

Plant checklist: Basil is now at its peak. Pinch back the plants every two or three days to keep them productive. Hang bunches of basil to dry, and make pesto to freeze. Preserve a good supply of other herbs by freezing, drying, and making flavored vinegars—already the days are growing shorter and nights are cooling off.

Autumn

As late-season splendors grace the autumn garden, finish harvesting and start putting the garden to bed.

SEPTEMBER This month sometimes brings our most beautiful weather, so treat yourself to a picnic in the garden while you can. Many fruits and vegetables reach their peak harvest, and herbs are still in good supply for use in preserving them.

Garden checklist: Early in the month, sow annual winter rye for green manure. Rake and shred falling leaves and start a new compost heap. Test your soil and apply lime as needed. Lay out and prepare new beds to get a head start on spring.

Plant checklist: Make a last sowing of arugula. Pickle cucumbers with dill, shallots with rosemary, and beans with tarragon. I like to make up giant batches of tomato sauce and minestrone soup with lots of herbs and freeze them for winter meals. Harvest ripe seeds of arugula, calendula, chives, cilantro, dill, fennel, lemon balm, lovage, nasturtium, sage, sweet cicely, savory, and others. Pick basil as long as you can, then pull up or turn under plants.

OCTOBER Harvesting is slowing down, the growing season is nearly over, and putting the garden to rest before heavy rains and frost arrive becomes a priority. Much of the work you accomplish in October will pay dividends in labor saved during the spring.

Garden checklist: Continue work on new and established beds. Sprinkle open beds with long-term soil amendments such as lime and rock phosphate before digging or tilling them. Try to rid your perennials of weeds, especially grasses, which will otherwise resume their pernicious growth in January. Cover beds with a layer of straw, lawn clippings, or shredded leaves. Like green manures, these mulches help keep down weeds and prevent nutrients from leaching from your soil. By spring the mulch will turn into rich, crumbly humus.

Plant checklist: Dig scented geraniums, pot in damp peat moss, and bring them into the greenhouse, garage, or porch for the winter. Bring in bay trees potted in a rich soil mix (check leaves for scale insects). Water plants sparingly throughout the winter and watch for aphids and other bugs. If you grew French lavender, bring in plants to bloom during the holidays. Take in 1- and 2-year-old rosemary plants to ensure winter survival.

Plant garlic. Cut down the stalks and seed heads of perennials such as fennel and lovage. Pull out basil, calendula, and other spent annuals or shear them with a lawn mower and add the clippings to your compost bin. Once the ground has been deeply moistened by autumn rains, divide and move perennials.

Light frosts, expected by the middle of the month, gradually become sharper until a killing frost zaps tender plants. Protect cilantro, baby dill, sweet marjoram, and summer savory from frost with spun-bonded polyester row covers.

WINTER

The quiet days of winter can be very productive. The seasoned gardener knows that these months are ideal for planning and preparing next year's garden. Rest is also important.

NOVEMBER The rains begin, but there still may be time to do some of the tasks you could not get to earlier. If it is too wet and cold to garden, keep warm indoors and catch up your gardening journal while the past season is still fresh in your mind.

Garden checklist: Dig finished compost and spread it 2 inches thick around the base of perennials such as rosemary—it will not only protect plants from winter cold but nourish them when spring growth begins. Start ordering catalogs.

Plant checklist: Continue moving and dividing perennials if you have not done so; get your garlic planted.

DECEMBER Your dried and preserved herbs now add a personal touch to holiday meals and gifts. Garlic braids, herb vinegars, and bundles or wreaths of dried herbs are always appreciated. Rosemary and bay trees make lovely Christmas trees; French lavenders, scented geraniums, and other plants brought inside also make a beautiful display. Seed catalogs begin arriving for your perusal.

Garden checklist: Take a break. If the weather is mild, you may have a chance to do a little weeding and mulching.

Plant checklist: Harvest rosemary, fresh sage, thyme, and winter savory from your garden.

January This month rest, dream, plan, and lay the foundation for the coming year. The preparation you do even when the garden is frozen will make everything go more smoothly later. Read your herb and garden books and store up ideas for future reference. Many seed catalogs are informative sources about growing herbs and new varieties. Plan and organize, mend tools, and get little jobs done now, before the busy time of sowing, transplanting, weeding, and harvesting arrives.

Garden checklist: Check the straw mulch on your garlic and apply more if necessary. Keep an eye on any plants wintering indoors and water them sparingly.

Clean out your greenhouse, sterilize used pots in a solution of 1 tablespoon of bleach per gallon of water, or set up an area indoors for seedlings. Write out plant markers when you have time.

Plant checklist: Go through and organize seeds you purchased or collected last year. Order new seeds before the spring rush. Spray scented geraniums and bay trees with insecticidal soap for aphids and scale. In case of a serious cold snap, throw an old blanket over your rosemary plants at night and bring your most cherished tender plants indoors temporarily. Knock heavy snow off perennials, especially lavenders, to keep the branches from splaying or breaking.

Dig and pot a few plants of chives, parsley, and tarragon in a good potting soil. Water well with regular solution fish fertilizer and keep indoors or in the greenhouse. You will be enjoying a harvest of fresh herbs before your garden is producing.

February It is always a pleasure to watch the stirrings of spring in February. The region's Northwest Flower and Garden Show, held in Seattle in midmonth, is an extravaganza not to be missed. Attend excellent seminars, discover dozens of garden-related businesses and organizations, and be inspired by the beautiful gardens that give you a preview of spring. Finish up seed orders this month to be sure choice varieties are still available and seeds arrive before you need them.

Garden checklist: If the weather is fine, begin garden cleanup—rake leaves, pick up fallen branches, and pile plant debris on the compost heap. This is your last chance to plant that garlic!

Plant checklist: Cut back dead stalks of lemon balm, mint, oregano, tarragon, and other perennials with clippers or a string trimmer. Prune back woody sage plants and spread a handful of all-purpose fertilizer beneath each plant—they will bush out beautifully. Get a head start on pulling weeds—the earlier the better. If quack grass and other harmful weeds are invading chives, tarragon, or other perennials, dig the plants up and gently tease the grass roots out. If the problem is really severe, plan to start new, weed-free plants in a different location soon.

Purchase or mix your potting soil. Indoors, sow seeds of chives, garlic chives, lemon balm, lovage, parsley, thyme, and other herbs to move outside while the weather is still cool. Cut back scented geraniums by half to keep them from getting spindly. For commercial greenhouses, February is a peak season, as seedlings of all kinds are readied for marketing to your garden.

Appendixes

Regional Destinations

Gardeners in the maritime Northwest can gain information and inspiration from a marvelous variety of public and private herb gardens. You can borrow on the experience of knowledgeable herb growers by observing the ways they have solved design challenges and combined or highlighted certain herbs.

The display gardens of various institutions, estates, and businesses—each with its own character and focus—are intended for public enjoyment and education. Generally the larger ones are most accessible, but smaller gardens, which may be open for only a few hours a week, are well worth the extra effort to visit. It's a good idea to call and double-check on hours of business. Some interesting gardens are located at restaurants and inns that raise fresh herbs and greens for the kitchen while creating pleasant havens for guests. Another appealing model is the community garden, which combines the resources and styles of many individuals.

The farms and gardens listed all feature herbs and herbal products. As well as plants and seeds, many offer books, classes, and other educational opportunities. Remember, plants transported from either side of the Canada–United States border must be inspected.

BARN OWL NURSERY. 22999 SW Newland Road, Wilsonville, OR 97070; (503) 638-0387. *Chris and Ed Mulder. Follow the owl signs through rural countryside to this lovely place. You will find herb gardens (including an old-fashioned knot garden), a gift shop, classes, and a fine selection of plants, especially lavender and rosemary. Open April to July, Wednesday through Sunday, 10 a.m. to 5 p.m., and mid-September to mid-December, Wednesday and Sunday, 10 a.m. to 5 p.m.*

CEDARBROOK HERB FARM. 986 Sequim Avenue S, Sequim, WA 98382; (206) 683-7733. *Toni and Terry Anderson. Washington's oldest herb farm, which specializes in everlasting flowers and unusual garlics, also offers the Bell House gift shop, plants, a mail-order seed list, and classes. Open March 1 to December 24, 9 a.m. to 5 p.m., daily except Thanksgiving.*

DUTCHMILL HERBFARM. 6640 NW Marsh Road, Forest Grove, OR 97116; (503) 357-0924. *Barbara Remington lives, breathes, and wears lavender. In addition to common and unusual herb plants, the display gardens include 93 varieties of lavender. Open Wednesday through Saturday, noon to 6 p.m., and by appointment.*

ELDERFLOWER HERB FARM. 501 Callahan Road, Roseburg, OR 97470; (503) 672-7766. *John and Kelly Stelzer. This couple specializes in dried organic culinary herb blends and herb vinegars. Call for an appointment to see the production gardens; weekends are best.*

FAIRIE HERBE GARDENS. 6236 Elm Street SE, Tumwater, WA 98501; (206) 754-9249. *Dave Baird and Steve Taylor. You will find fragrant and medieval paradise gardens, unusual plants, "Fairie Balm" ointment, and more on this half-acre city lot. Open March 15 to October, Tuesday through Friday, 10 a.m. to 4 p.m.; Saturday and Sunday, 1 to 6 p.m.*

FAIRLIGHT GARDENS. 30904 164 SE, Auburn, WA 98002; (206) 631-8932. *Judy and Don Jensen. Discover display gardens, herbal and garden gifts, and plants; bamboo is also a specialty. Open April to November, Wednesday through Sunday, 10 a.m. to 6 p.m.*

FOXGLOVE HERB FARM. 6617 Rosedale Street, Gig Harbor, WA 98335; (206) 851-7477. *Ms. Michael Burkhart. This intimate, artful garden surrounding a log house–cum–gift shop is filled with topiaries and other garden delights. Ask about classes. Open Wednesday through Sunday, 10 a.m. to 5 p.m., mid-April through September.*

HAPPY VALLEY HERBS. 3497 Happy Valley Road, Victoria, BC, Canada V9C 2Y2; (604) 474-5767. *Lynda and Mike Dowling. Plants, display gardens, lavender beds, and market production fields flourish on 3 acres. Open Tuesday through Sunday, 12:30 to 5 p.m., April through September.*

HERBAN RENEWAL. 10437 19th Avenue SW, Seattle, WA 98146; (206) 243-8821. *Janice and Joe Peltier. Little lawn can be seen among these herb gardens, created with the Peltiers' "No Till, Sheet Mulch Method." Low mounds and curving beds are packed with a tremendous variety of herbs, espaliered Asian pears, and much more to demonstrate how productive a* city lot can be. Purchase plants and take advantage of classes, garden design services, and a basil festival in August. Open April through October, Thursday through Saturday, 11 a.m. to 5 p.m.

THE HERBFARM. 32804 Issaquah–Fall City Road, Fall City, WA 98024; (206) 784-2222. Ron Zimmerman and Carrie Van Dyke. Meander through 17 theme gardens and a working kitchen garden at the region's largest herb farm, east of Seattle, Washington. Classes, festivals, fine dining, and mail order also available. Open April to September, 9 a.m. to 6 p.m. daily; October to March, 10 a.m. to 5 p.m. daily.

HUMMINGBIRD FARM. 2041 N Zylstra Road, Oak Harbor, WA 98277; (206) 679-5044. Dave and Linda Harry. Visit the gorgeous display gardens and 2½ acres of herbs, then select from everlastings, cut flowers, dried flowers in bunches, and arrangements. Open eleven months; January by appointment. Tuesday through Saturday 9:30 a.m. to 6:30 p.m.; Sunday, 11 a.m. to 5 p.m.

LAKEWOLD. 12317 Gravelly Lake Drive, Tacoma, WA 98499; (206) 584-3360. Friends of Lakewold. This spectacular private garden is now open to the public; its Elizabethan knot garden, designed with culinary herbs as ornamentals, is worth the trip. Visit the beautiful gift shop and avail yourself of guided and self-guided tours. Open April to September; Thursday through Monday, 10 a.m. to 3:30 p.m.; Sunday, 1:00 to 3:30 p.m.

RAVEN HILL HERB FARM. 1330 Mt. Newton Road, Sannichton, BC, Canada V0S 1M0; (604) 652-4024. Noel Richardson, who presides over "rooms" of herb gardens overlooking a peaceful valley, has written two popular herb cookbooks. Open April to August, Sunday only, noon to 5 p.m.

ROVER'S. 2808 E Madison, Seattle, WA 98112; (206) 325-7442. Thierry Rautureau. This herb garden, beside French chef Rautureau's Seattle restaurant, holds 45 varieties of herbs, 15 edible flower varieties, and choice vegetables — all for the restaurant. You are welcome to visit the garden Tuesday through Saturday, 3 to 10 p.m.

SEATTLE TILTH ASSOCIATION. 4649 Sunnyside Avenue N, Seattle, WA 98103; (206) 633-0451. The meandering, clearly labeled community gardens at Seattle's Good Shepherd Center are connected by colorful mosaic pathways. Nearby are composting demonstrations, a solar greenhouse, community (P-patch) gardens, and the Tilth Office, which offers information on organic gardening. The spring plant sale features organic starts of many herbs and vegetables. Call for details about the September Harvest Fair. The main gardens are always open; the children's garden closes at dusk. The office is open Monday through Friday, 9 a.m. to 5 p.m.

SILVER BAY HERB FARM. 9151 Tracyton Boulevard, Bremerton, WA 98310; (206) 692-1340. *Mary Preus. Both theme and production gardens flourish at this peaceful farm on the shores of Puget Sound. Plants, seeds, and herbal or garden-oriented products are available in the gift shop. Open March 15 to December 23, Tuesday through Saturday, 11 a.m. to 5 p.m.; open Sunday, 11 a.m. to 5 p.m. June through September, and December.*

SOOKE HARBOR HOUSE. 1528 Whiffen Spit Road, RR 4, Sooke, BC, Canada V0S 1N0; (604) 642-3421. *Sinclair and Fredricka Phillip welcome you to one of the 10 best inns in Canada. The grounds are planted with herbs, vegetables, and native edible plants used in their superb restaurant. Open year-round.*

TERRITORIAL SEED COMPANY. 20 Palmer Avenue, Cottage Grove, OR 97424; (503) 942-9547. *Herb and vegetable starts, seeds, and gardening supplies are available at the company store. Gardens are open March to June, Monday through Saturday, 8 a.m. to 5:30 p.m.; Sunday 9 a.m. to 4 p.m. Organic methods are used in their trial gardens in London Springs, OR; call for directions. Open July to mid-September, Saturday, 1 to 4 p.m. Check the mail-order catalog for directions.*

UNIVERSITY OF BRITISH COLUMBIA PHYSIC GARDEN. 6804 SW Marine Drive, Vancouver, BC, Canada; (604) 822-9666. *This medieval medicinal herb garden, containing about 75 medicinal herbs, is a small part of the 72-acre University of British Columbia Botanic Garden, a teaching and research institution. The gift shop has dried flowers and some plants. Open daily except Christmas for a small entrance charge, 10 a.m. to 5 p.m. (11 a.m. to 5 p.m. in winter).*

UNIVERSITY OF WASHINGTON MEDICINAL HERB GARDEN. University of Washington Department of Botany, KB-15, Seattle, WA 98195; (206) 543-1126. *The plants grown in this garden were originally used by students in the College of Pharmacy to produce medicines. This much-loved garden, now maintained by volunteers, has more than 600 varieties of medic-*

inal and other useful plants. Free tours are available the second and fourth Sunday of the month, noon to 1 p.m. Open daily.

VanDusen Botanical Garden. 5251 Oak Street, Vancouver, BC, Canada V6M 4H1; (604) 266-7194. *A Mediterranean garden uses herbs such as chives, creeping thyme, lemon balm, and lavender as ornamentals. A small formal herb garden features fennel, French lavender, oregano, and various thymes, among others. Ornamental herbs can also be enjoyed in the Alma VanDusen Garden. Seeds are sold on the premises; call about the two yearly plant sales. Open daily except Christmas (for an entry fee), 10 a.m. to dusk.*

Verdi's Farm. 10325 Airport Way, Snohomish, WA 98290; (206) 568-0319. *Mike and Sue Verdi. Stop at the Verdi's farm stall in Seattle's Pike Place Market for herb plants in spring and check on the date of their annual farm festival, held on a Sunday in mid- to late August.*

Herb-Buying Directory

Mail-order seeds and plants can be obtained from sources throughout the maritime Northwest.

ABUNDANT LIFE SEED FOUNDATION. PO Box 772, Port Townsend, WA 98368; (206) 385-5660, Fax (206) 375-7445. *Dedicated to preserving open-pollinated seed varieties and native plants of the maritime Northwest, this nonprofit organization carries an excellent variety of herb seeds and books. Many of the seeds available through the catalog are grown organically here. Catalog, $2 suggested donation.*

ELDERFLOWER HERB FARM. 501 Callahan Road, Roseburg, OR 97470; (503) 672-7766. *Write or call for a free catalog of organically grown herb products.*

THE HERBFARM. 32804 Issaquah–Fall City Road, Fall City, WA 98024; (206) 784-2222, Fax (206) 789-2279. *The extensive free catalog of classes and products is an herb lover's delight.*

NICHOLS GARDEN NURSERY. 1190 N Pacific Highway, Albany, OR 97321. (503) 928-9280, Fax (503) 967-8406. *This mail-order gem offers a remarkable selection of herb seeds and plants, vegetables, flowers, tools, supplies, and more. Free catalog.*

RICHTERS. Goodwood, Ontario, Canada L0C 1A0; (416) 640-6677, Fax (416) 640-6641. *Known as Canada's herb specialists, this company offers a staggering array of seeds, plants, dried herbs, books, and more. Free catalog.*

SHEPHERD'S GARDEN SEEDS. 6116 Highway 9, Felton, CA 95018; (408) 335-6910. *Carefully chosen herb and salad seeds and plants complement the vegetable and flower selections in this distinctive catalog. Call their office for expert advice on horticultural questions. Catalog, $2.*

SILVER BAY HERB FARM. 9151 Tracyton Boulevard, Bremerton, WA 98310; (206) 692-1340. *A simple catalog of selected items available from the gift shop is $1.00, refundable with purchase.*

TERRITORIAL SEED COMPANY. PO Box 157, Cottage Grove, OR 97424; (503) 942-9547. *Specializing in seeds for the maritime Northwest, the current (free) catalog offers many herb varieties, plus several edible flowers and good growing information.*

Sources

Societies and Advice

AMERICAN HERBALIST GUILD. c/o Roy Upton, 3411 Cunnison Lane, Soquel, CA 95073; (408) 438-6851.

THE HERB SOCIETY OF AMERICA. 9019 Kirtland-Chardon Road, Mentor, OH 44060; (216) 256-0514.

INTERNATIONAL HERB GROWERS AND MARKETERS. 1202 Allanson Road, Mundelein, IL 60060; (708) 949-HERB.

COOPERATIVE EXTENSION SERVICE. *Each county in the United States has a representative of the state agricultural college. Their offices offer a wealth of information on growing and preserving herbs and other crops. Check your telephone book for Cooperative Extension under County listings.*

Bibliography

Adams, James. LANDSCAPING WITH HERBS. Portland, OR: Timber Press, 1987.

Blumenthal, Mark, ed. THE HERBALGRAM JOURNAL. Austin, TX: American Botanical Council.

Boxer, Arabella, and Philippa Back. THE HERB BOOK. New York: Gallery Books, 1988.

Bremness, Lesley. THE COMPLETE BOOK OF HERBS. London and New York: Penguin Group, 1988.

Dickson, Nancy, Richard Thomas, and Robert Kozlowski. COMPOSTING TO REDUCE THE WASTE STREAM. Ithaca, NY: Northeast Regional Agricultural Service, 1991.

Dille, Carolyn, and Susan Belsinger. HERBS IN THE KITCHEN. Loveland, CO: Interweave Press, 1992.

Engeland, Ron L. GROWING GREAT GARLIC. Okanogan, WA: Filaree Productions, 1992.

Foster, Steven. HERBAL BOUNTY: THE GENTLE ART OF HERB CULTURE. Layton, UT: Peregrine Smith Books, 1984.

Garland, Sarah. THE HERB GARDEN. London: Penguin Books, 1984.

THE HERB COMPANION. Loveland, CO: Interweave Press. *This periodical is published six times a year.*

Hillers, Val, ed. MASTER FOOD PRESERVER VOLUNTEER HANDBOOK. Pullman, WA: Washington State University, 1993.

Hoffman, David. THE NEW HOLISTIC HERBAL. Rockport, MA: Element Books, 1990.

Huxley, Anthony, Mark Griffiths, and Margot Levi, eds. THE NEW ROYAL HORTICULTURAL SOCIETY DICTIONARY OF GARDENING. New York: The Stockton Press, 1992.

James, Tina, Barbara Steele, and Marlene Lufriu. LOVELY LAVENDER. Littlestown, PA: Alloway Gardens, 1990.

Keville, Kathi. THE ILLUSTRATED HERB ENCYCLOPEDIA. New York: Mallard Press, 1991.

Kirkpatrick, Debra. USING HERBS IN THE LANDSCAPE. Harrisburg, PA: Stackpole Books, 1992.

Koepsell, Paul A., and Jay Pscheidt, eds. PACIFIC NORTHWEST PLANT DISEASE CONTROL HANDBOOK. Corvallis, OR: Oregon State University 1993. *Companion versions of this series cover insect and weed control.* Kowalchick, Claire, and William H. Hylton, eds.

RODALE'S ILLUSTRATED ENCYCLOPEDIA OF HERBS. Emmaus, Pa: Rodale Press, 1987.

Mabey, Richard, ed. THE NEW AGE HERBALIST. London: Gaia Books, 1988.

Ogden, Ellen. GROWING AND USING BASIL. Bulletin A-119. Pownal, VT: Storey/Garden Way Publishing, 1990.

Phillips, Roger, and Nicky Foy. THE RANDOM HOUSE BOOK OF HERBS. New York: Random House, 1990.

Readers' Digest Association. MAGIC AND MEDICINE OF PLANTS. Pleasantville, NY: 1986.

Simmons, Adelma G. HERB GARDENING IN FIVE SEASONS. New York: E. P. Dutton, Inc., 1964.

Stuart, Malcolm. THE ENCYCLOPEDIA OF HERBS AND HERBALISM. New York: Crescent, 1979.

Swanson, Faith, and Virginia Rady. HERB GARDEN DESIGN. Hanover, NH: University Press of New England, 1984.

More Reading

To obtain a free selected list of the most current books on herb gardening, compiled by Valerie Easton, Librarian, Elisabeth C. Miller Horticultural Library, University of Washington Center for Urban Horticulture, send a stamped, self-addressed legal-size (#10) envelope to: **Cascadia Gardening Series, Sasquatch Books, 1008 Western Avenue, Seattle, WA 98104.**

Index

Did you enjoy this book?

Sasquatch Books publishes high-quality books and guides related to the Pacific Northwest. Our books are available at bookstores and other retail outlets throughout the region. To receive a Sasquatch Books catalog, or to inquire about ordering our books by phone or mail, please contact us at the address below. Here is a partial list of our current titles.

GARDENING

Cascadia Gardening Series:

Water-Wise Vegetables
Steve Solomon

North Coast Roses
Rhonda Massingham Hart

Winter Ornamentals
Daniel Hinkley

The Border in Bloom
A Northwest Garden Through the Seasons
Ann Lovejoy

The Year in Bloom
Gardening for All Seasons in the Pacific Northwest
Ann Lovejoy

Growing Vegetables West of the Cascades
Steve Solomon's Complete Guide to Natural Gardening, 3rd Edition
Steve Solomon

Gardening Under Cover
A Northwest Guide to Solar Greenhouses, Cold Frames, and Cloches
William Head

Winter Gardening in the Maritime Northwest
Cool Season Crops for the Year-Round Gardener
Binda Colebrook

FOOD AND COOKING

The City Gardener's Cookbook
Totally Fresh, Mostly Vegetarian, Decidedly Delicious Recipes from Seattle's P-Patches
Edited by P-Patch Cookbook Committee

Northwest Wines
A Pocket Guide to the Wines of Washington, Oregon, and Idaho
Paul Gregutt and Jeff Prather

Carla Emery's Old Fashioned Recipe Book
The Encyclopedia of Country Living, 9th Edition
Carla Emery

Pike Place Market Cookbook
Recipes, Anecdotes, and Personalities from Seattle's Renowned Public Market
Braiden Rex-Johnson

The Good Food Guide to Washington and Oregon
Discover the Finest, Freshest Foods Grown and Harvested in the Northwest
Edited by Lane Morgan

Recipes from the San Juan Islands
A Giftbook Collection
Greg Atkinson

Seasonal Favorites from The Herbfarm
A Giftbook Collection
Ron Zimmerman and Jerry Traunfeld

Eight Items or Less Cookbook
Fine Food in a Hurry
Ann Lovejoy

GUIDEBOOKS

Northwest Best Places
Restaurants, Lodgings, and Touring in Oregon, Washington, and British Columbia
Edited by David Brewster and Stephanie Irving

Seattle Best Places
The Most Discriminating Guide to Seattle's Restaurants, Shops, Hotels, Nightlife, Sights, Outings, and Events
Edited by Stephanie Irving

Seattle Survival Guide
The Essential Handbook for Urban Living
Theresa Morrow

SASQUATCH BOOKS

1008 Western Avenue, Suite 300 • Seattle, WA 98104
(206) 467-4300